55 Tactics
for Implementing
RTI
in Inclusive Settings

Pam Campbell
Adam Wang
Bob Algozzine

CORWIN
A SAGE Company

For information:

Corwin
A SAGE Company
2455 Teller Road
Thousand Oaks, California 91320
(800) 233-9936
Fax: (800) 417-2466
www.corwinpress.com

SAGE Ltd.
1 Oliver's Yard
55 City Road
London EC1Y 1SP
United Kingdom

SAGE India Pvt. Ltd.
B 1/I 1 Mohan Cooperative
    Industrial Area
Mathura Road, New Delhi
India 110 044

SAGE Asia-Pacific Pte. Ltd.
33 Pekin Street #02-01
Far East Square
Singapore 048763

Printed in the United States of America.

Library of Congress Cataloging-in-Publication Data

Campbell, Pam, 1942-
55 tactics for implementing RTI in inclusive settings / Pam Campbell, Adam Wang, Bob Algozzine.
    p. cm.
Includes bibliographical references and index.
ISBN 978-1-4129-4239-3 (cloth : alk. paper)
ISBN 978-1-4129-4240-9 (pbk. : alk. paper)
    1. Remedial teaching. 2. Inclusive education. I. Wang, Adam, 1956- II. Algozzine, Robert. III. Title.
IV. Title: Fifty-five tactics for implementing RTI in inclusive settings.

LB1029.R4C354 2010
371.9'043—dc22   2009023351

This book is printed on acid-free paper.

09 10 11 12 13 10 9 8 7 6 5 4 3 2 1

Acquisitions Editor:	David Chao
Editorial Assistant:	Sarah Bartlett
Production Editor:	Eric Garner
Copy Editor:	Paula L. Fleming
Typesetter:	C&M Digitals (P) Ltd.
Proofreader:	Susan Schon
Indexer:	Molly Hall
Cover Designer:	Rose Storey

55 Tactics
for Implementing
RTI
in Inclusive Settings

To all teachers and those they teach . . .

Contents

Preface

As students with disabilities and learning differences are included in general education settings in greater numbers and for longer periods of time, educators—expert and novice alike—are searching for ways to meet these students' needs most effectively. While many recognize that a teacher's expertise is often the critical determinant in any student's achievement, they also realize that meeting the increasingly diverse needs of students calls for additional information and support. In this context, response to intervention (RTI) has emerged as a promising practice for both identification and prevention of the "most vulnerable, academically unresponsive children" in schools and school districts (Fuchs & Deshler, 2007, p. 131). According to Bradley, Danielson, and Doolittle (2007), the popularity of RTI is based partly on the promise that "teachers no longer would have to wait for students to fail before the students could receive services" (p. 8) and partly in the pledge of change at the first indication of unresponsiveness to classroom implementations of scientifically based interventions. (See Figure 1: RTI Model on page viii.)

RTI is "a multitier prevention model that has at least three tiers" (Bradley et al., 2007, p. 9) or levels of intervention provided in response to increasing needs of students. Regular assessments and progress monitoring are prominent in RTI and establish the importance of using proactive identification of students experiencing difficulties for different tiers of intervention and support (Fuchs & Deshler, 2007). Primary (Tier I) interventions are designed to address the majority of students' instructional needs. If a student has been identified as needing additional support, RTI directs the use of evidence-based, "secondary" (Tier II) interventions, which are easy to administer to small groups of students and which require limited time and staff involvement. Tertiary (Tier III) intervention is specifically designed and customized instruction that is extended beyond the time allocated for Tiers I and II; in some states, Tier III intervention means the provision of special education services. Figure 1 depicts the RTI tiers.

When implementing RTI in a setting (see Table 1 on page ix: RTI Overview), teachers need easy and simple access to authentic information about effective teaching and instructional practices. (See www.ed.gov [search "RTI"] and www.whatworksclearinghouse.org.)

When using the RTI tiers as the framework for determining the appropriate structure and setting for each student, teachers must design instruction to address the student's current learning phase appropriately. In this way, students can move from Accuracy, to Proficiency, to Maintenance, and finally Generalization of skills. The Instructional Planning and Learning Phases Chart (see Table 2 on page x) can be used to guide planning and instruction.

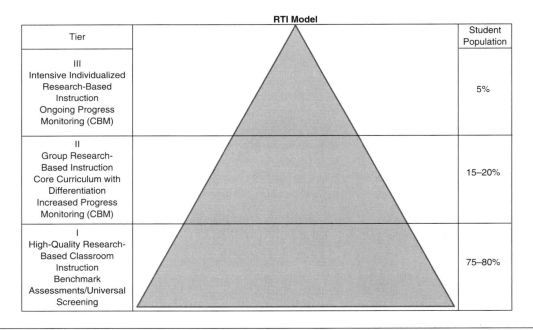

RTI Model

Tier		Student Population
III Intensive Individualized Research-Based Instruction Ongoing Progress Monitoring (CBM)		5%
II Group Research- Based Instruction Core Curriculum with Differentiation Increased Progress Monitoring (CBM)		15–20%
I High-Quality Research- Based Classroom Instruction Benchmark Assessments/Universal Screening		75–80%

Figure 1   RTI Model

Overview

55 Tactics for Implementing RTI in Inclusive Settings is the third book in our collection of evidence-based practices designed to help teachers address the instructional needs in America's classrooms. As with the other books in the series, it is organized around four components of instruction (planning, managing, delivering, and evaluating), and it is based on our fundamental belief that teachers can respond to instructional diversity more effectively when provided with an easily accessible resource of effective tactics (cf. Algozzine & Ysseldyke, 1992; Algozzine, Ysseldyke, & Elliott, 1997).

This book differs a bit because we believe that most effective evidence-based practices (tactics) can be modified to meet the instructional needs of *all* learners across categories of disability, grade levels, and content areas in the context of RTI. Thus, we have eliminated those distinctions in this book. We have retained "learning differences" as a marker for providing information teachers need to teach effectively in inclusive settings. We have also added "RTI tier accommodations/modifications" to each tactic to guide teachers in adapting tactics to support RTI practices and meet individual instructional needs across levels and tiers of instruction.

Accommodations are changes in the ways in which students access information and demonstrate understanding; accommodations do not alter the content of instruction, just the methods used in the instructional and evaluation processes (Walsh, 2001). Commonly used accommodations include books on tape, enlarged print, untimed tests, and communication boards. *Modifications*, on the other hand, do change the content of student learning and are typically substantiated by an Individualized Education Program (IEP) plan (e.g., an alternate curriculum or different instructional goals for a particular unit or period of instruction). Selecting appropriate accommodations and modifications depends on collaboration among special and general educators, access to materials and resources, research, and common sense.

Table 1   RTI Overview

Guiding Principles: Focus on the general education curriculum, progress monitoring, early intervention, and the use of evidence-based practices. May be used to identify students with Specific Learning Disabilities (SLD) for special education services.

	Tier 1	Tier II	Tier III
Students	All	Targeted (Unsuccessful in Tier I)	More specifically targeted (Unsuccessful in Tiers I and/or II)
Instructor	General Education Teacher	General Education Teacher Specialists (reading, speech/language)	General Education Teacher Special Education Teachers: (Resource, Special/Language Clinicians, etc.)
Location	General Education Classroom	Various locations	Various locations
Intensity	Daily instruction in language arts (reading, oral & written language), mathematics	Specified frequency: Hours per day: 5–10 Days per week: 3–4 Specified duration: # weeks (9–12)	Most intensive Frequency: based on student need Duration: minimum 12 weeks
Grouping Arrangements	Large and small groups Peers Independent	Small Group (2–5)	Small Group and Individualized
Monitoring	Focus: adequate progress in general education curriculum Universal screening (3 times per year or periodically) throughout the year	Focus: remediation of skill deficits 1–3 times per week	Focus: student learning daily
Curriculum	General Education	General Education	General Education or Alternative
Instruction	High quality, developmentally appropriate, differentiated instruction	Targeted instruction to remediate specific skill deficits	More specifically targeted instruction to meet the needs of individual learners

Table 2 Instructional Planning and Learning Phases

	ACQUISITION	PROFICIENCY/ AUTOMATICITY	MAINTENANCE	GENERALIZATION
Goal	To increase probability of correct response **Skill Introduction**	To maintain high frequency, to correct frequency, to correct response, to develop high rates of correct responding **Skill Mastery**	To maintain high frequencies and rates over time **Independence**	To maintain high frequencies, rates over time, and across situations **Application**
Learner Characteristics	Naive Unskilled Low accuracy/low speed	High accuracy and speed	High accuracy and speed	High accuracy and speed
Instructional Characteristics	Intense Teacher/Student interaction	Fading Teacher/Student interaction	Fading Teacher/Student interaction	Fading Teacher/Student interaction Increased application across other natural environments

Instruction	**Teacher** **Student**
	
	model imitate
	demonstrate respond
	explain
	examples/
	nonexamples
	prompt
	guide
	cue
	feedback:
	(corrective/supportive)
		Teacher **Student**
		
		fading drill
		intermittent fast pace
		reminders Practice
		              massed
		          Guided to
		          Independent
			Teacher **Student**
			
			fade cues drill
			detail fast pace
			prominence Independent
			time Practice
			intermittent
			reminders
				Instruction imbedded in other activities
				
				natural antecedents
				high utility
				natural consequences

Content	**Introduction & Practice with:** Definitions Concepts characteristics Procedures	**Additional Practice with:** Definitions Concepts characteristics Procedures	**Review of:** Definitions Concepts characteristics Procedures	**Applications of:** Definitions Concepts characteristics Procedures
Measurement	Accuracy Frequency of correct/errors	**Accuracy and Speed** Frequency of correct/errors Rate of responding	**Accuracy and Speed** Frequency of correct/errors Rate of responding	**Accuracy and Speed** Frequency of correct/errors Rate of responding
Cue	**Do It**	**Do It Faster**	**Use It or Lose It**	**Use It Again Somewhere Else**

SOURCE: Algozzine, B., Campbell, P., & Wang, A. (2009a). *63 tactics for teaching diverse learners: Grades 6-12*. Thousand Oaks, CA: Corwin.

x

55 Tactics for Implementing RTI in Inclusive Settings provides all teachers (regardless of level, experience, or area specialization) with access to effective instructional tactics that can be used across multiple levels of intervention. The book was developed using a peer review process that encouraged flexibility and resulted in a collection of teaching tactics to enable teachers to meet the needs of diverse students, classrooms, and schools. It is based on sound, evidenced-based models of instruction, and its structure encourages the identification and use of effective practices. *55 Tactics for Implementing RTI in Inclusive Settings* includes practices that are effective for students with or without disabilities at all grade levels. It provides a foundation for the leveled intervention recommended as best practice within RTI models being implemented in America's schools.

Ecological Validity

Ecological validity refers to the extent to which the underlying constructs of an educational model are grounded in logical, representative, and important conditions within the real world of schools. It is a measure of the value, worth, or projected effectiveness of the model. The ecological validity or usefulness of *55 Tactics for Implementing RTI in Inclusive Settings* is grounded in five assumptions:

1. All children want to learn.
   Ask any child.

2. All children can learn.
   Ask any parent.

3. All schools can educate diverse groups of students.
   Ask any administrator.

4. All classrooms are places where students with varying instructional needs can learn.
   Ask any teacher.

5. All teachers want to teach well so students will learn and succeed; all they need is time, access to information, and sustained support.
   Ask anybody.

Underlying Model

55 Tactics for Implementing RTI in Inclusive Settings is based on a practical model in which four components serve as the base for a set of organizing principles of effective instruction (see below).

Components and Principles of Effective Instruction

Component	Principle
Planning	Decide What to Teach
	Decide How to Teach
	Communicate Realistic Expectations
Managing	Prepare for Instruction
	Use Time Productively
	Establish Positive Environments

Component	Principle
Delivering	Present Information
	Monitor Presentations
	Adjust Presentations
Evaluating	Monitor Student Understanding
	Monitor Engaged Time
	Keep Records of Student Progress
	Use Data to Make Decisions

To bring the model to life and address the ever-present concern of administrators and teachers for implementation assistance, each component and principle is embodied by a set of strategies that represents plans for action in putting theory into practice (see example below).

Components, Principles, and Strategies of Effective Instruction

Component	Principle	Strategy
Planning	Decide What to Teach	Assess to Identify Gaps in Performance
		Establish Logical Sequences of Instruction
		Consider Contextual Variables
	Decide How to Teach	Set Instructional Goals/Establish Performance Standards
		Choose Instructional Methods and Materials
		Establish Grouping Structures
		Pace Instruction Appropriately
		Monitor Performance and RePlan Instruction
	Communicate Realistic Expectations	Teach Goals, Objectives, and Standards
		Teach Students to Be Active, Involved Learners
		Teach Students Consequences of Performance

Strategies are steps that should be taken to implement principles and components of effective instruction (i.e., the "what" rather than the "how" of teaching). *Tactics* are actions that a teacher can take to influence learning (i.e., the "how" of effective teaching). They are the lowest level a component can be broken into for instructional purposes; they are specific behaviors or teaching activities (see below).

Organizational Relations in Algozzine and Ysseldyke Model

Component	Delivering Instruction
Principle	Providing Relevant Practice
Strategy	Provide Students with Help
Tactic	Use Signals to Request Help: Develop a signal for each student to use when assistance is needed during an independent practice session. Circulate through the room when students are practicing and look for signs that someone needs help. Provide help as quickly as possible so that students can continue to work.

This model of effective instruction has been translated into a collection of evidence-based tactics to help teachers respond to individual differences common in America's classrooms. The information in *55 Tactics for Implementing RTI in Inclusive Settings* was drawn from review of professional publications, as well as from extensive observations of experienced teachers and other professionals who teach students with disabilities and diverse learning needs in general education classrooms. The tactics are grouped according to the components and principles of effective instruction identified by Algozzine and Ysseldyke (1992), and they are presented in a consistent format. In this book, 8 of the 63 strategies have been integrated into a single tactic—thus, 55 tactics.

In addition, tactics have reviews by other educators as to their use, as well as references to the literature to provide evidence of their effectiveness. A reproducible checklist of accommodations/modifications and a worksheet for planning and implementing RTI accommodations/modifications are provided in Appendixes A and B, respectively; a worksheet for documenting RTI accommodations/modifications is provided in Appendix C. Finally, in addition to References and Additional Readings, we have provided Selected Internet Resources related to accommodations/modifications.

Where to Go From Here

Every day, teachers are faced with questions that must be addressed if they are to be effective with all children.

> I teach students in an elementary school. My specialty is history and mathematics. How can I develop appropriate learning activities for a student with learning disabilities? How can I arrange my instruction to accommodate students with a deficit in short-term memory? How can I improve my ongoing assessment of student learning? How do I use data to make decisions?

55 Tactics for Implementing RTI in Inclusive Settings is based on a fundamental belief: teachers can respond to instructional diversity more effectively when provided with an easily accessible resource of effective tactics. *55 Tactics for Implementing RTI in Inclusive Settings* responds to two fundamental problems in education: regardless of certification area, (1) very few teachers receive sufficient experience during student teaching or practicum experiences in identifying or using evidence-based tactics of effective instruction, and (2) very few teachers receive instruction in or have access to specific tactics for addressing instructional diversity and meeting individual needs in their classrooms.

55 Tactics for Implementing RTI in Inclusive Settings helps teachers to associate a problem with an easily accessible set of solutions. It is unique in that we not only provide classroom-tested tactics for effective instruction but we also substantiate them with relevant and related literature. Thus, teachers can be assured of implementing evidence-based practices grounded in ongoing research. We also provide feedback, comments, and examples from practicing teachers, who offer practical suggestions as to how tactics might be modified and/or enhanced in terms of their content or application. In addition, we have suggested RTI accommodations/modifications for each tactic and included related worksheets to assist teachers in implementing tactics. Many tactics are clearly applicable across RTI Tiers I and/or II and/or III. If, for example, a tactic were effective in a Tier III instructional setting, teachers would simply need to modify it for effective use in Tiers I or II. The same holds true as students move in and out of Tiers I, II, and III. Effective teaching strategies/tactics that are evidence/research based have multiple applications across instructional settings and learners.

Most teachers agree: they often do not have enough time to meet all the needs of all their students effectively. Thus, time is an ongoing and primary need. *55 Tactics for Implementing RTI in Inclusive Settings* addresses this need by providing teachers with quick access to reliable information about effective instructional tactics, regardless of their area of expertise or the diverse needs of their students. When using *55 Tactics for Implementing RTI in Inclusive Settings*, teachers have several options: identifying a problem and searching for solutions using the model of effective instruction, searching the database without referencing a problem or any aspects of it, examining the knowledge base underlying each tactic, saving items from the database for later use, implementing tactics, and evaluating and revising instructional plans using information in the database. This easy and simple access to authentic information about effective teaching and instructional practices promotes effective implementation of RTI.

For some teachers, the need to accommodate the individual learning needs of an increasingly diverse population of students is daunting. Focusing on critical instructional planning and learning phases as well as primary, secondary, and tertiary responses to instruction will

- benefit all students (including those who do not have a disability);
- apply across content areas, grade levels, and settings;
- address a student's learning style (possibly described in an IEP);
- provide ample opportunities for change and modification; and
- *enable students to learn and be successful.*

Acknowledgments

No one writes a book without help and support from others, and we are no exception. When we began this project, our goal was to share what we had learned from working with teachers and their students around the country. We are thankful for that experience and for what they and our own students continually taught us. In particular, we are grateful to Cynthia Ayon, Ruth Devlin, Tina Guard, Shannon Hennrich, Mike Henry, Paula Laub, Dustin Mancl, Nichola Perrilo, Jerry Raso, Rene Segler, Ima Jean Turner, Sean Tyler, and John Yoder for their thoughtful, expert, and valuable contributions. We are also grateful to our colleagues, who by way of conducting and reporting their research have provided an ever-renewing resource of evidence-based practices for enabling diverse learners to succeed in school. We further acknowledge the very professional support of David Chao, Brynn Saito, Sarah Bartlett, Eric Garner, and Kathleen McLane at Corwin; they kept us on track and contributed greatly to every part of producing this book.

About the Authors

Pam Campbell, PhD from University of Florida, is an associate professor in the Department of Special Education at the University of Nevada, Las Vegas (UNLV). During her 35 years as an educator, she has taught university courses in instruction, assessment, curriculum, and classroom management for both general and special educators. In addition, she has been a public school teacher in general education, Chapter I, and special education classrooms. She served in the dual role of university professor and coordinator of seven Professional Development Schools (PDS) at the University of Connecticut and currently at UNLV is coordinator of the Paradise PDS. Her research interests focus on linking the preparation of teacher candidates and sustained professional development of practicing teachers through technology. Her work has been published in *TEACHING Exceptional Children, Remedial and Special Education, Record in Educational Leadership, The Professional Educator,* and the *Council for Administrators of Special Education.* She is also the coauthor of *Improving Social Competence: Techniques for Elementary Teachers.* In addition, together with the coauthors of this book, she has published *63 Tactics for Diverse Learners: K–6* and *63 Tactics for Diverse Learners: Grades 6–12.* She has served the field of special education through numerous local, state, regional, and national presentations; as field reviewer for *Exceptional Children,* the *Journal of Special Education Technology, TEACHING Exceptional Children,* and *Teacher Education and Special Education;* and, currently, as coeditor of *School-University Partnerships: The Journal of the National Association of Professional Development Schools.*

Jianjun (Adam) Wang, MA from University of Connecticut, is senior instructional technology specialist at Williams College. He has been responsible for collaborating with Campbell, Algozzine, and James Ysseldyke in the design and development of STRIDE, a database program that provided the framework for the contents of this book. He has also been instrumental in the implementation of STRIDE in the preparation of future teachers, as well as the ongoing professional development of practicing educators. In addition, together with the coauthors of this book, he has published *63 Tactics for Diverse Learners: K–6* and *63 Tactics for Diverse Learners: Grades 6–12.* He has served as an instructor in technology courses and made several regional, national, and international conference presentations related to the effective implementation of technology in education. His research interests concern how educational technology can enhance human learning and focus on developing Web-based learning and teaching tools to enhance the undergraduate learning experience.

Bob Algozzine, PhD from Penn State University, is codirector of the Behavior and Reading Improvement Center and professor of educational administration, research, and technology at the University of North Carolina at Charlotte. He is the coauthor of *Strategies and Tactics for Effective Instruction, Critical Issues in Special and Remedial Education, Introduction to Special Education,* and other college textbooks. In addition, together with the coauthors of this book, he has published *63 Tactics for Diverse Learners: K–6* and *63 Tactics for Diverse Learners: Grades 6–12.* He has published more than 250 articles on effective teaching, assessment, special education issues, and improving the lives of individuals with disabilities. His recent research has been published in the *High School Journal,* the *Journal of Educational Research,* and *Teacher Education and Special Education.* He has been a special education classroom teacher and college professor for more than 30 years in public schools and universities in New York, Virginia, Pennsylvania, Florida, and North Carolina. For nine years, he was coeditor, with Martha Thurlow, of *Exceptional Children,* the premier research journal in the field of special education. He is currently the coeditor of *Teacher Education and Special Education, The Journal of Special Education,* and *Career Development for Exceptional Individuals.*

Planning Instruction

Effective teachers carefully plan their instruction. They decide what to teach and how to teach it. They also communicate their expectations for learning to their students. In this part of our resource, we describe evidenced-based strategies for each principle of planning instruction.

Component	Principle	Strategy
Planning Instruction (Part I)	Decide What to Teach (Chapter 1)	Assess to Identify Gaps in Performance
		Establish Logical Sequences of Instruction
		Consider Contextual Variables
	Decide How to Teach (Chapter 2)	Set Instructional Goals/Establish Performance Standards
		Choose Instructional Methods and Materials
		Establish Grouping Structures
		Pace Instruction Appropriately
		Monitor Performance and RePlan Instruction
	Communicate Realistic Expectations (Chapter 3)	Teach Goals, Objectives, and Standards
		Teach Students to Be Active, Involved Learners
		Teach Students Consequences of Performance

Planning Instruction Works: A Case Study

There are so many things that I consider as I plan long-term, weekly, and daily lessons. Because I work with language learners who range from being emergent English speakers to almost completely bilingual and academic levels that range from on grade level to two or three years below, all my instruction must be differentiated—designed to meet the children at their current academic levels and RTI tier—while addressing district mandated curricular goals. I use content to teach language and strive to engage all my students in meaningful activities that give them the opportunity to construct meaning.

In my planning, I include a daily variety of Tier I (whole-group) and Tier II (small-group) instruction. In addition, I collaborate with a special education teacher and paraprofessional to provide Tier III instruction that is targeted specifically to meet students' educational needs. My small groups are flexible depending on the activity— sometimes they are ability groups, and other times they are specifically designed to include a variety of language levels, reading abilities, writing abilities, and/or oral proficiency levels. I find that routine helps the students learn how to be responsible for their own learning. While we work at sticking to our agenda, however, I know that it is important to allow space for the teachable moments that arise. I use the writing of my students as well as my own planned objectives to design writing workshop lessons. My readers' workshop and math instruction find students working with small groups of like-ability peers, as well as having the opportunity to work with classmates above or below that student's level.

While my goals are high, I recognize that all children learn at different speeds, in different ways, and design my teaching accordingly.

—Ruth Devlin
Elementary School Teacher

1

Decide What to Teach

Component	Principle	Strategy
Planning Instruction	Decide What to Teach	Assess to Identify Gaps in Performance
		Establish Logical Sequences of Instruction
		Consider Contextual Variables

Chapter 1: **Decide What to Teach**

Strategy:	**Assess to Identify Gaps in Performance**
Learning Difference:	Cognition Mixed; Attention; Study Skills; Processing Visual Information; Memory Short-term; Memory Long-term; Self-confidence; Cognition Low; Cognition High; Processing Verbal Information; Receptive Language/ Decoding (listening, reading); Expressive Language/Encoding (speaking, writing, spelling)

Tactic Title:	**Testing the Limits of Assessments**
Problem:	Teachers use the results of tests/quizzes/assessments to determine "what to teach." Therefore, it is often frustrating when students perform poorly on assessments, especially on a multiple-choice test where responses are limited and require only the recognition of information.
Tactic:	First, give students a multiple-choice test. Grade the test. Give students the opportunity to discuss their correct and incorrect responses with their peers and you. This discussion could include their perceptions of the "best" possible answer to each item on the test and how they reached those conclusions. Allow students to use information from texts, notes, and other sources. You can choose to monitor and include conversations in determining the final grade.
Example:	I've never totally relied on just a test score or a letter grade when I am deciding what to teach next. At the very least, I do a task analysis of the test and my students' responses to each item [See Task Analysis: Assessment worksheets below]. Sometimes, I have individual conferences to determine why they responded as they did. I may not retest the exact same material; however, as a result, I do know what they need to learn. Great tactic! *Amalio T., teacher*
Benefits:	Testing the limits of assessment results • allows students to think about and defend their answer selections; • provides students with motivation to understand, analyze, and synthesize testing procedures and their thinking processes; • helps students learn to question and to debate answers; • enables students to become involved and motivated to gain "extra points" and improved grades; • contributes to the students' motivation, participation, and understanding; • enables teachers to measure the depth of students understanding and involvement; and • provides a tool for teachers to evaluate students and their performance in an authentic way that facilitates students' involvement.

RTI Accommodations/Modifications:

> *Tiers I & II:* Provide

- tests-on-tape;
- extended time;
- altered test format to include both open- and closed-ended question formats; and/or
- questions aligned with Bloom's taxonomy (revised) and student abilities (see Assessment Planner).

> *Tier III:* In addition, provides

- smaller units of information;
- additional prompts/visual cues;
- daily progress monitoring and immediate feedback; and/or
- charts for visual analysis of student performance.

Literature:

Algozzine, B., Campbell, P., & Wang, A. (2009a). *63 tactics for teaching diverse learners: Grades 6–12.* Thousand Oaks, CA: Corwin.

Algozzine, B., Campbell, P., & Wang, A. (2009b). *63 tactics for teaching diverse learners: K–6.* Thousand Oaks, CA: Corwin.

Anderson, L. W., & Krathwohl, D. R. (Eds.). (2001). *A taxonomy for learning, teaching, and assessing: A revision of Bloom's taxonomy of educational objectives* (abridged). New York: Longman.

Hoover, J. J. (2009). *RTI: Assessment essentials for struggling learners.* Thousand Oaks, CA: Corwin.

Yunker, B. D. (1999). Adding authenticity to traditional multiple-choice test formats. *Education, 120,* 82–87.

Task Analysis: Assessment

Directions:

Step 1: Use this first worksheet to complete a task analysis of each test/quiz item. A sample entry* is provided.

Title of Test/Quiz/Examination:_____ Date:_____

Item #	Knowledge/Skills Needed	Format	Input	Output	Time Limitations
* 14	Recognition of state capitals	Multiple-choice	Written	Written	Yes

Task Analysis: Assessment

Step 2: List the instructional abilities/needs of specific students. Compare with your Task Analysis (Step 1). Make an alternative plan to "test the limits" to assess the actual knowledge of those students. A sample entry* is provided.

Student	Learning Strengths	Learning Difference(s)	Accommodations Needed	Test the Limits by . . .
* Sami	Fine motor skills Auditory processing	Visual memory	Information delivered orally	Providing a taped version of the test

Chapter 1: **Decide What to Teach**

Strategy:	**Establish Logical Sequences of Instruction**

Learning Difference: *Attention; Study Skills*

Tactic Title:	**Using The T-G-I-F Model**

Problem: Student with learning differences frequently have "skill deficits" or "learning differences" that affect their ability to perform certain tasks in the classroom.

Tactic: The T-G-I-F model presents a well-organized process of instruction that addresses the deficits of students with ADD.

T: **Teacher-directed instruction:** Present and model new information and ask questions to probe for student understanding. Promote active participation by the students and provide immediate positive feedback and supportive informative error correction.

G: **Guided practice instruction:** Provide structured activities for the students to practice new skills.

I: **Independent practice activities:** Provide activities, such as enrichments or labs, that lead to extended practice of skills.

F: **Final measurement:** Continuously monitor student understanding. Keep ongoing records of student progress and teach students how to keep track of their own progress.

Example: The T-G-I-F model is an excellent model for instruction in any classroom—general or special education, inclusive or not. However, in my inclusive general education classroom, I've found that I need to make modifications for individual students, according to their learning differences. In some instances, I might need to seat the student closer to me, while in others, I would pair the student with a peer or paraprofessional. It all depends on the needs and abilities of my students. But that's what makes teaching so exciting, isn't it?

Schranda C., teacher

Benefits: Using the T-G-I-F model

* provides just enough structure and immediate feedback to students with attention issues;
* enables all students to succeed; and
* incorporates evidenced-based, effective instructional practices into an easy-to-remember acronym (TGIF).

RTI: Accommodations/Modifications:

Tiers I & II: Provide

- preferential seating;
- peer tutoring; and/or
- a variety of guided and then independent practice activities that are aligned with individual student strengths.

Tier III: In addition, provides

- additional modeling and scaffolding;
- faster-paced and more specific skills instruction; and/or
- additional cues/prompts.

Literature:

Hudson, P. (1997). Using teacher-guided practice to help students with learning disabilities acquire and retain social studies content. *Learning Disabilities Quarterly, 20,* 23–32.

Jung, L. A., Gomez, C., Baird, S. M., & Gaylon Keramidas, C. L. (2008). Designing intervention plans: Bridging the gap between individualized education programs and implementation. *TEACHING Exceptional Children, 41*(1), 26–33.

Kemp, K., Fister, S., & McLaughlin, P. J. (1995). Academic strategies for children with ADD. *Intervention in School and Clinic, 30,* 203–210.

Kroesbergen, E. H., Van Luit, J. E. H., & Mass, C. J. M. (2004). Effectiveness of explicit and constructivist mathematics instruction for low-achieving student in the Netherlands. *Elementary School Journal, 104,* 233–251.

Chapter 1: Decide What to Teach

Strategy:	**Consider Contextual Variables**

Learning Difference: Low Self-confidence

Tactic Title:	**Integrating a Social Curriculum Into Daily Instruction**

Problem:

Many students come to school with less social competence than their peers. They just do not know acceptable social behaviors or how to use them. In addition, they may have difficulty managing their feelings in socially appropriate ways. Therefore, these students frequently lack close, stable relationships with caring adults and typically struggle establishing appropriate peer relationships.

Tactic:

Use a "Morning Meeting" every day to create stability, consistency, and community and foster responsive interactions through the designated periods of Greeting, Sharing, Activity, and News & Announcements. Next, set up relaxation centers, where students who are being disruptive or uncooperative can go to "defuse" (by focusing on specific academic activities). Teach students how to prioritize problems and solutions from the lowest scale, first among peers and then by involving the principal or other authority figure as a last resort. Teach students how to resolve dilemmas within the classroom by modeling and coaching via simulations.

Example:

Many students lack the caring and support of family and their community and do indeed come into school with their books and frustrations. I've always believed that my credibility as a teacher relies on establishing a safe place for learning—both academic and social. If we can't solve our own issues as a community in our own setting, then I've failed my students. Being a wise and caring educator is expected for any student but is absolutely imperative for those less fortunate students who do not have caring role models at home.

Cody T., teacher

Benefits:

Infusing a social curriculum into the context of daily instruction

- can meet the needs of students who lack age-appropriate social skills;
- utilizes an instructional process that integrates social and academic goals; and
- creates a sense of social responsibility and community that can extend beyond the classroom.

RTI Accommodations/Modifications:

> *Tier I:*
>
> - Match simulation topics to the specific needs in students in your class(es) (for example, for individual students, how to enter a group; for the class as a whole, how to deal with anger);
> - establish and enforce rules and expectations consistently; and/or
> - be totally aware of *all* of your students *all* of the time.
>
> *Tier II:*
>
> - Provide activities in centers that match individual student needs;
> - use music;
> - teach stress management skills and self-talk; and/or
> - organize groups that include students with different levels of social skill.
>
> *Tier III:*
>
> - Use instructional materials that incorporate individual student needs/ interests into academic goals;
> - use think-alouds to model thinking in responding to social concerns;
> - use Positive Peer Reporting; and/or
> - provide immediate corrective/supportive feedback.

Literature:

Applebaum, M. (2009). *The one-stop guide to implementing RTI: Academic and behavioral interventions, K–12.* Thousand Oaks, CA: Corwin.

Campbell, P., & Siperstein, G. N. (1994). *Improving social competence: A resource for elementary school teachers.* Boston: Allyn & Bacon.

Christensen, L., Young, K. R., & Marchant, M. (2004). The effects of a peer-mediated positive behavior support program on socially appropriate classroom behavior. *Education and Treatment of Children, 27,* 199–234.

Meadan, H., & Monda-Amaya, L. (2008). Collaboration to promote social competence for students with mild disabilities in the general classroom: A structure for providing social support. *Intervention in School and Clinic, 43,* 158–167.

More, C. (2009). Digital stories targeting social skills for children with disabilities: Multidimensional learning. *Intervention in School and Clinic, 43,* 168–177.

2

Decide How to Teach

Principle	Strategy
Decide How to Teach	Set Instructional Goals/Establish Performance Standards
	Choose Instructional Methods and Materials
	Establish Grouping Structures
	Pace Instruction Appropriately
	Monitor Performance and RePlan Instruction

Chapter 2: **Decide How to Teach**

| *Strategies:* | **Set Instructional Goals/Establish Performance Standards** |

Learning Difference: Attention; Self-control; Processing Verbal Information

| *Tactic Title:* | **The Majority Rules** |

Problem: Students often fail to pay attention to instruction because they do not see how a lesson or activity relates to them. Consequently, they are less apt to participate and be successful. We need to engage students in making decisions about their learning. While curriculum standards and benchmarks frame most of what we teach, we can always find creative ways to present and vary instruction to meet our students' interests and instructional needs.

Tactic: Review the topic/goal/learning objectives with students, why they are important, and the relevance to their learning. Then, discuss the responsibilities of being a citizen in a democracy, the importance of participation and debate, and the concept of the majority vote. Next, have students as a group create a list of appropriate subtopics. Record and display their list and discuss the merits of each item. Give students the opportunity to debate pros and cons with one another. Then, have students vote on each topic; make them responsible for tallying the votes and determining the collective course of action. Finally, post the instructional goals and expectations for performance.

Example: Students are most intellectually engaged when they help define lesson content, have to pursue an interesting direction, are allowed different forms of expression, create original and public products, and accomplish a socially relevant task. They are writing letters, text messaging, researching, collaborating, and creating exceptional products to demonstrate their learning. Teaching this way has changed my "instructional life," while energizing and totally involving my students in their learning. My students have learned that everyone's views are respected. Now we all have a sense of control, creativity, and freedom.

Lidia H., teacher

Benefits: Using democratic principles and involving students in the determination of instructional goals and establishing performance standards

- gains student attention;
- makes lessons relevant because lesson structures are decided collectively; and
- provides a way to align required content with the expertise and preferences of a competent teacher.

RTI Accommodations/Modifications

Tiers I & II: Provide

- different ways for students to express their understanding/learning;
- additional time for students to "wonder" and find their own individual ways to learn; and/or
- interesting new grouping configurations based on student needs, abilities, and interests.

Tier III: In addition, provide

- very specific tasks and roles for students;
- learning goals and objectives that are aligned with the general education curriculum to the greatest degree possible; and/or
- modified modes of presentation and student responding.

Literature:

Chorzempa, B. F., & Lapidus, L. (2009). "To find yourself, think for yourself": Using Socratic discussions in inclusive classrooms. *TEACHING Exceptional Children, 41*(3), 54–59.

Jung, L. A., Gomez, C., Baird, S. M., & Gaylon Keramidas, C. L. (2008). Designing intervention plans: Bridging the gap between individualized education programs and implementation. *TEACHING Exceptional Children, 41*(1), 26–33.

Perone, V. (1994). How to engage students in learning. *Educational Leadership, 52*(5), 11–13.

Soder, R. (1995). *Democracy, education, and the schools.* San Francisco: Jossey-Bass.

Soder, R., Goodlad, J. I., & McMannon, T. J. (2001). *Developing democratic character in the young.* San Francisco: Jossey-Bass.

Chapter 2: **Decide How to Teach**

Strategy:	**Choose Instructional Methods and Materials**

Learning Difference: Short-term Memory, Long-term Memory

Tactic Title:	**Using "Foldables" to Teach Vocabulary**

Problem: As students progress through elementary and secondary school, they need to continue to expand their vocabulary. However, many struggle with learning new words and remembering their definitions.

Tactic: Give each student the "Making a Foldable" worksheet (below) and a list of vocabulary words and their definitions. Tell students to write each definition in a space in the right-hand column. Then, students cut into the left-hand column on dotted lines, from the left to the center. Direct students to fold each flap carefully over the definition and write the corresponding vocabulary word on the top of the flap. Students can then use the Foldable to study vocabulary words and their definitions. With the Foldable closed, students can read the word and try to recall the definition; with the Foldable open, they can read the definition and try to recall the vocabulary word.

Example: My students love Foldables. They enjoy making them and studying with them. I love Foldables because they are easy to make and fit in their notebooks, so they take them home for extra practice. I use file folders to make the Foldables sturdier. With the folder closed, I cut vertically from bottom to top, in the center. Then I tape the two parts that have been cut off to make a second Foldable. Sometimes, they practice with a peer, sometimes, they practice when they've finished a task early, and sometimes we play team games with the Foldables. In addition, their quiz scores have improved dramatically.

Frieda L., teacher

Benefits: Using foldables to teach vocabulary

- involves students in the process of making their own materials;
- promotes maintenance and generalization;
- motivates students to practice frequently; and
- provides an excellent tool for peer and whole-class activities.

RTI Accommodations/Modifications:

Tiers I, II, & III:

- Use different words for individual students according to their specific needs;
- provide words in a student's native language and definitions in English (or vice versa); and/or
- use foldables to teach math facts, picture/word recognition, names of colors and shapes, historical dates/events, book titles/author, and other memorization tasks.

Literature: Bender, W. N., & Larkin, M. J. (2009). *Reading strategies for elementary students with learning difficulties: Strategies for RTI.* Thousand Oaks, CA: Corwin.

Brown, J. E., & Doolittle, J. (2008). A cultural, linguistic, and ecological framework for response to intervention with English language learners. *TEACHING Exceptional Children, 40*(5), 66–72.

Davis, G. N., Lindo, E. J., & Compton, D. L. (2007). Using graphic organizers to attain relational knowledge from expository text. *Journal of Learning Disabilities, 35,* 306–320.

Hudson, P., Miller, S., & Butler, F. (2006). Integrating reform-based mathematics and explicit teaching in inclusive classrooms. *American Secondary Education, 35,* 19–32.

Miller, S. P., & Hudson, P. (2007). Using evidence-based practices to build mathematics competence related to conceptual, procedural, and declarative knowledge. *Learning Disabilities Research & Practice, 22,* 47–57.

Schnakenberg, J. W. (2009). A synthesis of reading interventions and effects on reading comprehension outcomes for older struggling readers. *Review of Educational Research, 79,* 262–300.

Making a "Foldable"

Directions: List definition of each vocabulary word in right-hand column.

Cut on horizontal dotted lines (from left to center line).

Fold left column over right column (on center line), covering definitions.

Write vocabulary word on the outside of corresponding flap.

Chapter 2: **Decide How to Teach**

Strategy:	**Establish Grouping Structures**

Learning Difference: Self-control

Tactic Title:	**Improving Social Skills Through Group Work**

Problem: Many students with disabilities receive more individualized instruction in a self-contained classroom, resource room, or learning center. When they are included in a general education setting, they face both academic and social challenges. Cooperative group structures can address both needs simultaneously.

Tactic: First, organize small groups of students whom you've selected very carefully. You might structure your groups based on diverse learning abilities / needs, diverse levels of social competence, which students could serve as appropriate role models for their peers, or some other factor. You could use the Grouping Chart, Parts 1 & 2, (below) to determine which students would like to work with one another. Provide a task for the group and assign each student an appropriate role: recorder, timekeeper, reporter, materials organizer, etc. When students have completed the academic task, have them review their process of working together: What helped the group? What hindered the group? What might they do next time? How well did they do? And so forth. As the groups are working, circulate around the classroom and make notes regarding individual students and groups.

Example: I've used cooperative groups for many years. Now, with many more students with disabilities being placed in my classroom, arranging instruction so that my students must work cooperatively to succeed is an excellent tool for accommodating a variety of student abilities and learning differences. I give students roles that play to their strengths and abilities, while simultaneously challenging them. Cooperative groups have really helped my students learn to get along with their peers; there is much less tension and much more kindness in my classroom today.

Cyndi R., teacher

Benefits: Using cooperative groups enables teachers to

- monitor academic learning and peer interactions simultaneously;
- use student-centered learning; and
- "jigsaw" content by giving each group responsibility for one portion of an academic assignment and for teaching the other groups.

RTI Accommodations/Modifications:

Tiers I, II, & III:

- Individualize materials and responsibilities according to student abilities;
- provide taped versions of instructions; and/or
- vary the requirements of the assignment (length, output format, etc.).

Tiers II & III: In addition,

- use small-group and individual instructional opportunities to preteach and role-play cooperative learning activities;
- provide graphic organizers of lesson content and roles; and/or
- model appropriate behavior for students.

Literature:

Campbell, P., & Siperstein, G. P. (1994). *Developing social competence: A resource for elementary teachers.* Boston: Allyn & Bacon.

Fore, C., III, Riser, S., & Boon, R. (2006). Implications of cooperative learning and educational reform for students with mild disabilities. *Reading Improvement, 43*(1), 3–12.

Fuchs, L. S., & Fuchs, D. (2007). A model for implementing responsiveness to intervention. *TEACHING Exceptional Children, 39*(5), 12–20.

Marzano, R. J., Pickering, D. J., & Pollack, J. E. (2001). *Classroom instruction that works: Research-based strategies for increasing student achievement.* Alexandria, VA: Association for Supervision and Curriculum Development.

Slavin, R. E. (2000). *Cooperative learning: Theory, research, and practice.* (2nd ed.). Boston: Allyn & Bacon.

Grouping Chart

(Part 1)

Directions: List student names alphabetically in the "Student Names" column. Ask students to select one of the three other columns ("Very Much," "OK," "Preferably No") to choose peers with whom they would like to collaborate. Give one sheet to each student in the class.

Student Names	1 Very Much	2 OK	3 Preferably No

SOURCE: Algozzine, B., Campbell, P., & Wang, A. (2009a). *63 Tactics for teaching students with diverse needs: Grades 6–12.* Thousand Oaks, CA: Corwin.

Grouping Chart

(Part 2)

Directions: Enter student names in Column 1 (vertically) and Row 1 (horizontally) in alphabetical order. Using individual student worksheets (Part 1), begin with student 1 in Column 1. Working horizontally, enter that student's ratings (1–3) for all classmates (from left to right). Note: There will be no ratings entered in the box that corresponds vertically and horizontally for a particular student. Total ratings horizontally to see what one student thinks about others. Total ratings vertically to see what other students think about a student. Review totals carefully to determine which students would work together well, which students need a classmate who would be willing to work with them, and which students are willing to work with others. Repeat this assessment periodically as relationships change.

Names / Names		T:(1)	T:(2)	T:(3)

(blank grouping chart grid with rows and columns, T(1):, T(2):, T(3): rows at bottom)

SOURCE: Algozzine, B., Campbell, P., & Wang, A. (2009a). *63 Tactics for teaching students with diverse needs: Grades 6–12.* Thousand Oaks, CA: Corwin.

Chapter 2: **Decide How to Teach**

Strategy:	**Pace Instruction Appropriately**

Learning Difference: Attention

Tactic Title:	**Break Regulation for Maintaining Quality Work Effort**

Problem: Many students find it difficult to focus on a task over an extended period of time. This tactic manages breaks and work quality on a long-term project.

Tactic: Set up a work and break schedule to enable students with attention difficulties to maintain their work quality throughout the day (see Assignment Schedule on page 24). When assigning a long-term project, divide the project into reasonable short-term objectives with specific interim deadlines. Then, as students proceed through the assignment, set individual objectives for each day's work (e.g., outline Chapter 1, finish three illustrations, find three credible resources, etc.). Sit with the students during the first work period to determine how long they can focus before the work quality begins to decline. At that point, allow these students to take a five-minute break (walk around, have a snack, read a book, etc.) after which the students return to the task for another work period. Students stop working on the project upon completion of the daily assignment and reaching the objective for that day.

Example: I've found that setting long-term goals and specifying short-term objectives really helps my students . . . not only those with attention issues but many others as well. I use a plan book. I keep a calendar. Why shouldn't my students learn this lifelong skill as well? When they get to middle and high school, they are going to have to juggle assignments and due dates across several content areas. So I believe it is essential to start now.

Sophia R., teacher

Benefits: Teaching organizational skills while individualizing the pacing of instruction

- can reduce interruptions to learning;
- improve the quality of student work; and
- teach students to take greater responsibility for their learning.

RTI Accommodations/Modifications:

Tiers I & II:

- Tape the daily schedule to student's desk;
- include space on the daily schedule for students to enter a start time and a finish time to enable them to learn how to budget their time more wisely; and/or
- assign peer buddies to encourage, motivate, and support each other.

Tier III:

- Break the assignment down into smaller, more manageable parts;
- provide daily checks on student progress toward completion of the assignment; and/or
- collaborate with other teachers/specialists to incorporate appropriate modifications to the assignment, based on the student's needs/abilities.

Literature:

Dollard, N. (1996). Constructive classroom management. *Focus on Exceptional Children, 29,* 1–12.

Ehri, L. C., Nunes, S. R., Stahl, S. A., & Willows, D. M. (2001). Systematic phonics instruction helps students learn to read: Evidence from the National Reading Panel's meta-analysis. *Review of Educational Research, 71*(3), 393–447.

Rademacher, J. A., Shumaker, J. B., & Deshler, D. D. (1996). Development and validation of a classroom assignment routine for inclusive settings. *Learning Disability Quarterly, 19,* 163–177.

Assignment Schedule

Name:_____   Date:_____   Class:_____

Time	Assignment	Comments	Initials

Source: Algozzine, B., Campbell, P., & Wang, A. (2009a). *63 tactics for teaching diverse learners: Grades 6–12.* Thousand Oaks, CA: Corwin.

Chapter 2: **Decide How to Teach**

Strategy:	**Monitor Performance and Replan Instruction**

Learning Difference: Self-confidence; Fine Motor (handwriting)

Tactic Title:	**Using Cards to Expand Vocabulary Knowledge**

Problem: Students often have difficulty studying and learning new vocabulary words because their handwriting is poor and, consequently, the definitions are difficult to decipher. In addition, having to correct their mistakes can lead to frustration.

Tactic: Students type each vocabulary word on one index card and its definition on another. Check their cards to be sure that students can read both the word and the definition. Next, students place word cards on a table or desk and place the correct definition on top of the word card. Check student progress and simply remove the definition card if it is with an incorrect word and encourage the student to try again. If students have repeated difficulty with specific matches, remove the word(s) and create a separate subset for additional practice. When students master the difficult matches, return the subset to the larger group of cards. Students repeat this game until they master the new vocabulary. Small envelopes or plastic bags are an easy way to store an individual student's cards.

Example: Using the computer to create vocabulary cards has enabled my students to focus on the purpose of the activity (learning new vocabulary) and not be limited or frustrated by their poor handwriting. I usually schedule practice times during the first or last few minutes of class when students may be particularly challenged to focus on work. Once they have mastered a vocabulary word or subset of words and definitions, I let them choose from several options to maintain their learning: find pictures to go with words, create a vocabulary collage or mobile, or videotape themselves acting out the word.

Ariel B., teacher

Benefits: Using legible cards to expand vocabulary knowledge

- gives students the opportunity to practice vocabulary words without having to overcome deciphering issues;
- lets the teacher easily monitor student learning, detect/correct errors, and replan instruction; and
- provides an accessible instructional tool that can be easily reproduced or modified.

RTI Accommodations/Modifications:

   Tiers I, II, & III:

- Provide a visual cue or keyword on the card to remind students of the definition of the vocabulary word;

- use peers to check other students' progress and provide supportive and/or corrective feedback; and/or
- select specific vocabulary words based on each student's needs.

Literature: Graham, S., Morphy, P., Harris, K. R., Fink-Chorzempa, B., Saddler, B., Moran, S., et al. (2008). Teaching spelling in the primary grades: A national survey of instructional practices and adaptations. *American Educational Research Journal, 45,* 796–825.

Uberti, H. Z., Scruggs, T. E., & Mastropieri, M. A. (2003). Keywords make the difference! Mnemonic instruction in inclusive classrooms. *TEACHING Exceptional Children, 35*(3), 57–61.

Wanzek, J., Vaughn, S., Wexler, J., Swanson, E. A., Edmonds, M., & Kim, A. (2006). A synthesis of spelling and reading interventions and their effects on the spelling outcomes of students with LD. *Journal of Learning Disabilities, 39,* 528–543.

3

Communicate Realistic Expectations

Principle	Strategy
Communicate Realistic Expectations	Teach Goals, Objectives, and Standards
	Teach Students to Be Active, Involved Learners
	Teach Students Consequences of Performance

Chapter 3: **Communicate Realistic Expectations**

Strategy:	**Teach Goals, Objectives, and Standards**

Learning Difference: Speaking/Talking; Attention; Study Skills; Social Knowledge; Self-control; Social Behaviors; Expressive Language/Encoding (speaking, writing, spelling); Fine Motor (handwriting, articulation, etc.); Gross Motor (running, walking, etc.)

Tactic Title:	**Teaching Students to Manage Their Behavior**

Problem: Frequently, students with behavioral problems are removed from the classroom when they are disruptive. While some teachers consider this a punisher, for some students leaving the classroom may actually be reinforcing. In addition, removing students also deprives them of opportunities to learn—both academically and behaviorally.

Tactic: Collaborate with other educators, the student, and the student's parents (if possible) to develop a list of specific behavioral objectives that are consistent across settings. Set up a point system and determine the period of time in which a point can be earned for appropriate behavior. Then, from the list, select 1–2 specific behavioral objectives. Some choose the most intrusive or problematic behaviors; others select the behaviors that the student can achieve most easily to give him or her the experience of being successful. Use the Student Interest Survey (on page 30) to determine academically-focused reinforcers for appropriate behavior. Use the Data Collection Sheet (on page 31) to monitor a student's behavior throughout the day and at home, if needed. If a student meets the behavioral objectives during a specified time period, that student earns points, which can be accumulated and traded in for a reinforcer. Initially, teachers/parents might determine whether objectives have been met. However, it is essential that this responsibility be given to the student at some point. As the student masters an objective, increase the time period and/or reduce the point values and exchange the reinforcers for those that are more natural (verbal praise, an encouraging e-mail message, etc.).

Example: This is an effective tactic to teach students how to manage their classroom behavior and, consequently, improve academic achievement. I graph the behavior of all students over time to analyze the effects of particular reinforcers and/or teaching strategies on my student's behavior. Involving them in the planning process—the selection of objectives, the determination of reinforcers, etc.—teaches them to take responsibility for their learning and behavior; it also gives them a greater sense of control, which is very motivating for them. Finally, I'm always very, very careful to be sure that my students know that it is the behavior that is "bad," not them.

Rahul J., teacher

Benefits: Teaching self-management to students

- is applicable across a wide range of students and behaviors;
- results in opportunities for greater appropriate participation in class-room activities; and
- accommodates students with behavioral issues more successfully in general education classrooms.

RTI Accommodations/Modifications:

Tiers I, II, & III:

- Implement a classwide intervention system that ensures close supervision/monitoring; provides feedback, error correction, and contingent praise; and increases student opportunities to respond.
- Laminate the Data Collection Sheet to reuse with other students and/or behaviors;
- modify time periods, reinforcers, point values, etc. according to student needs and achievements; and/or
- ask the student to complete a Data Collection Sheet as well and compare it with the teacher's analysis. Points can be given for "agreements."

Literature: Conroy, M. A., Sutherland, K. S., Snyder, A. L., & Marsh, S. (2008). Classwide interventions: Effective instruction makes a difference. *TEACHING Exceptional Children, 40*(6), 24–30.

Eber, L., Breen, K., Rose, J., Unizycki, R. M., & London, T. (2008). Wraparound as a tertiary-level intervention for students with emotional/behavioral needs. *TEACHING Exceptional Children, 40*(6), 16–22.

Mooney, P., Ryan, J. B., Uhing, B. M., Reid, R., & Epstein, M. H. (2005). A review of self-management interventions targeting academic outcomes for students with emotional and behavioral disorders. *Journal of Behavioral Education, 14,* 203–221.

Mullins, D. (1996). A quartet of success stories: How to make inclusion work. *Educational Leadership, 53,* 51–55.

Reid, R., Trout, A. L., & Schartz, M. (2005). Self-regulation interventions for children with attention deficit/hyperactivity disorder. *Exceptional Children, 71,* 361-377.

Student Interest Survey

Select from among the following to determine your students' interests. Having this information is extremely helpful in designing behavior management plans, determining appropriate consequences for classroom rules, and finding instructional materials and activities that will foster student learning.

I like to . . .

I really don't like to . . .

Working with others is . . .

Working by myself is . . .

In my free time, I . . .

My favorite subject is . . .

I admire . . .

I am afraid of . . .

I am really good at . . .

Books are . . .

Computers are . . .

I know how to . . .

I use computers to . . .

I wish I knew how to . . .

I like to read about . . .

I could teach other people to . . .

I want to know more about . . .

I want to learn how to . . .

I like it when my teacher . . .

I wish my teacher would . . .

I don't like to . . .

I like my best friend because . . .

I wish people would . . .

My favorite time in school is . . .

My favorite time at home is . . .

My family . . .

I wish I could . . .

I wish people knew that I . . .

My favorite animal is . . .

SOURCE: Algozzine, B., Campbell, P., & Wang, A. (2009b). *63 tactics for teaching diverse learners: K–6.* Thousand Oaks, CA: Corwin.

Data Collection Sheet

Student Name:_____   **Date:**_____

Behavioral Objective: _____

Time Period	Yes	No	Points
TOTALS:			

Chapter 3: **Communicate Realistic Expectations**

Strategy:	**Teach Students to Be Active, Involved Learners**

Learning Difference: Seeing; Processing Visual Information; Memory Long-term; Receptive Language/Decoding (listening, reading); Processing Verbal Information

Tactic Title:	**Strategies for Teaching Music to Blind Students**

Problem: Some teachers assume that blind students cannot be taught to read and understand music.

Tactic: Teaching blind students about music may begin 3–4 years after they have learned to read Braille, if not sooner. A number of publishers now produce music in Braille for the blind. These students may read their parts while singing or learn a piece phrase by phrase and then apply their knowledge to playing an instrument. Memorization will definitely be important in this instance, because both hands will be needed to hold and play the instrument. Another option is to have a student listen to music. It is very easy to transcribe music by ear and then imitate it on one's own. Play-along recordings also accompany most lesson books and allow students to hear models.

Example: I've been working with my student's general education teacher to figure out ways that we might align our instruction. We started out collaborating because I have one of her students who is blind in my music class. I told her about using prerecorded music for the student to model, and she immediately saw the similarity to taped books. So she's started using my tactic in her classroom to teach reading, which gives greater consistency to the student. In addition, the tactic is effective with other students as well. Now we're both using recordings of the student reading *and* playing the recorder to review and evaluate her learning. In fact, we now have a portfolio of her accomplishments this year to share with her parents.

Griffen T., music teacher

Benefits: Using this tactic

- affords blind students the opportunity to participate in an activity that others do;
- allows them to learn more about their own body's dexterity by learning an instrument and moving their hands, fingers, and muscles in their face and using their breath and breath support; and
- gives them a chance to learn about music and understand it by becoming a part of an ensemble and participating in musical events.

RTI Sample Accommodations/Modifications:

Tier I: Apply this tactic in other content areas and with other students by

- taping books and students' oral reading;
- using peer readers; and/or
- selecting reading materials that are specific to each student's reading level and interests.

Tiers II & III: Proceed as above and/or by

- teaching reading passages in smaller chunks;
- providing immediate supportive/corrective feedback; and/or
- using kinesthetic materials, such as sandpaper letters, to provide another modality for student learning.

Literature: Mazur, K. (2004). An introduction to inclusion in the music classroom. *General Music Today, 18*, 6–11.

McLeod, V. (1987). The teaching of music to primary children in schools for the visually handicapped compared with mainstream schools. *British Journal of Visual Impairment, 5*, 99–101.

Chapter 3: **Communicate Realistic Expectations**

Strategy:	**Teach Students Consequences of Performance**

Learning Difference: Attention; Self-control; Social Behaviors; Social Knowledge; Self-confidence

Tactic Title:	**Using Contingency Contracts With Students**

Problem: Sometimes, when students complete assignments before others, they use the remaining time inappropriately and disrupt the learning of their peers. Contingency contracts can be used to give students options for using their time more wisely.

Tactic: Together with the student, make a list of academic activities that the student would enjoy in the school setting (extra time at the computer, free reading, etc.). (See Student Interest Survey on page 30). List specific expectations for appropriate behavior in the classroom. Using the student's list of preferred activities, determine the rewards for displaying appropriate behavior, as well as the consequences for not displaying appropriate behavior. Finally, establish a time limit (e.g., every week) for fulfilling the contract. Enter these data on the Student Behavior Contract Sheet (on page 36). This gives the student a "clean slate." At the end of the established time period, review the contract with the student and determine whether a reward has been earned. Revise the contract as needed.

Example: Contingency contracts work for all students who need some guidance/structure in modifying their behavior. I like them because they are private and can be individualized according to the needs of any student, not just those with disabilities. However, my goal is to phase the contracts out. I do this by moving to naturally occurring reinforcers (social praise, extra academic credit, etc.) and by gradually giving the student full responsibility for making the evaluation. First I do it, then we do it together to see if we agree (and I give extra points for "agreements"), and then the student does it alone. In this way, I'm not only remediating inappropriate behavior, I am teaching the student to take responsibility for his or her behavior.

Victor M., teacher

Benefits: Contingency contracts

- are applicable across students, types of behavior (tardiness, fighting, attendance, study skills, etc.), and classrooms;
- provide a tool for teaching students to take responsibility for their own behavior; and
- clarify expectations and set limits for students.

RTI Accommodations/Modifications:

> *Tiers I, II, & III:*
>
> - Revise contracts when they are not working according to the predetermined schedule;
> - implement contracts across classrooms and content areas; and/or
> - use contracts as a communication tool with parents and caregivers.
>
> *Tiers II & III:*
>
> - Provide additional behavior prompts/cues;
> - increase use of praise and supportive feedback; and/or
> - teach students to self-monitor/record, self-evaluate, and self-reward.

Literature:

Din, F. S., Isack, L. R., & Rietveld, J. (2003, February–March). *Effects of contingency contracting on decreasing student tardiness.* Paper presented at the annual conference of the Eastern Educational Research Association, Hilton Head Island, SC.

Wilkinson, L. A. (2003). Using behavioral consultation to reduce challenging behavior in the classroom. *Preventing School Failure, 47*(3), 100–105.

Student Behavior Contract Sheet

_____

(Student Name)

I will behave in the following ways:

_____

_____

_____

_____

_____

My incentive will be:

_____

_____

_____

This contract will be renegotiated on:

_____

_____   _____

Student Signature   **Teacher Signature**

_____   _____

Today's Date   **Today's Date**

SOURCE: Algozzine, B., Campbell, P., & Wang, A. (2009a). _63 tactics for teaching diverse learners: Grades 6–12_. Thousand Oaks, CA: Corwin.

PART II

Managing Instruction

Effective teachers manage their instruction by preparing classrooms and learning materials to maximize the success of their students, by using instructional time productively, and by making classrooms positive learning environments. In this part of our resource, we describe evidence-based strategies for each principle of managing instruction.

Component	Principle	Strategy
Managing Instruction (Part II)	Prepare for Instruction (Chapter 4)	Set Classroom Rules/Communicate and Teach Classroom Rules
		Communicate Consequences of Behavior
		Handle Disruptions Efficiently
		Teach Students to Manage Their Own Behavior
	Use Time Productively (Chapter 5)	Establish Routines and Procedures
		Organize Physical Space
		Allocate Sufficient Time to Academic Activities
	Establish Positive Environments (Chapter 6)	Make the Classroom a Pleasant, Friendly Place
		Accept Individual Differences
		Establish Supportive, Cooperative Learning Environments
		Create a Nonthreatening Learning Environment

Managing Instruction Works: A Case Study

Being a new teacher has its challenges. Managing instruction in inclusion classrooms can be one of the greatest. But when effectively and efficiently done, it can be rewarding for both students and their teachers. Having just finished my first semester coteaching high school science in an inclusion classroom, I learned very quickly the importance of managing instruction. It was more a necessity than a luxury when facing a single class of over 44 freshmen, 39 of whom were boys. On the first day, I realized taking attendance could have taken up to one-fifth of the instruction time. So the next day, I implemented an alphabetized class list created on a spreadsheet for students to initial as they came in the door. Additionally, the graphic organizers, agendas, activity sheets, or PowerPoint notes were placed beside the sign-in sheet so students could pick them up as they came into the classroom.

I learned how to adapt my planning and teaching to meet the needs of students needing Tier I, II, or III instruction. I organized my classroom to accommodate small-group and individual instruction, as well as the introductory whole-group lesson. I provided individualized assignments, worksheets, and supplementary materials. My students learned the importance of routine and responsibility in an environment where they were supported and challenged.

—Tina Guard
High School Teacher
Special Education

Prepare for Instruction

Component	Principle	Strategy
Managing Instruction	*Prepare for Instruction*	*Set Classroom Rules/Communicate and Teach Classroom Rules*
		Communicate Consequences of Behavior
		Handle Disruptions Efficiently
		Teach Students to Manage Their Own Behavior

Chapter 4: **Prepare for Instruction**

Strategy:	**Set Classroom Rules/Communicate and Teach Classroom Rules**

Learning Difference: Attention; Social Knowledge; Self-control; Social Behaviors; Self-confidence

Tactic Title:	**Effective Rules and Routines**

Problem: Instructional time is often lost due to interruptions and disruptions, such as when students ask to get a drink of water, to go to the bathroom, and to sharpen a pencil. Therefore, it is important to establish and clarify rules and routines.

Tactic: Establish classroom rules and consequences on the first day of school. To empower students, include them in the decision-making process. Define consequences *both* for appropriate and for inappropriate behavior. Then, always follow through. Consistency and clarity are essential in the formation of respectful, trusting relationships and a smoothly operating classroom.

Example: Last year, at our first schoolwide staff development day, we focused on disruptive classroom behavior. First, as a large group, we developed a list of disruptive behaviors. Then, we divided into smaller groups where we discussed one behavior and our solutions or strategies for dealing with it. For example, one group talked about setting ground rules from the outset and dealing with disruptive students one-on-one. They thought that, because their students believed that they had a "voice" in their classroom, many of the problems associated with disruptive behaviors were resolved. Then, each group shared the results of their discussion; in total, we covered at least a dozen topics related to rules and routines. Finally, we agreed on schoolwide rules and procedures to provide consistency for our students across classrooms and settings.

Karel T., teacher

Benefits: Implementing rules and routines effectively

- lets students know what is expected of them, always;
- minimizes disruptions to instruction; and
- teaches students to assume responsibility for their actions, while demonstrating positive decision-making skills.

RTI Accommodations/Modifications:

Tier I:

- Post rules and consequences where they are easily seen;
- model and practice following classroom rules appropriately;
- develop "withitness" by scanning your students periodically and using physical proximity so that you are always aware of everything that is happening in your classroom; and/or
- teach consistent routines to ensure "smoothness and momentum."

Tiers II & III:

- Modify rules to address specific needs in small-group and/or one-on-one instructional arrangements;
- individualize contingencies; and/or
- increase use of contingent praise.

Literature:

Ellsworth, J. (1996). Enhancing student responsibility to increase student success. *Educational Horizons, 76*, 17–22.

Madsen, C. H., Jr., Becker, C. W., & Thomas, D. R. (2001). Rules, praise, and ignoring: Elements of elementary classroom control. *Journal of Direct Instruction, 1*(1), 11–25.

Marzano, R. J. (2003). *Classroom management that works: Research-based strategies for every teacher.* Alexandria, VA: Association for Supervision and Curriculum Development.

Sugai, G. (2008). *School-wide positive behavior support and response to intervention.* Retrieved April 9, 2009, from http://www.rtinetwork.org

Chapter 4: **Prepare for Instruction**

Strategy:	**Communicate Consequences of Behavior**

Learning Difference: Attention; Social Knowledge; Self-control; Social Behaviors

Tactic Title:	**Modifying Instruction for Students With Attention Issues**

Problem: Many students have difficulty focusing on instruction and learning activities. Consequently, their inability to stay on-task and respond appropriately can be disruptive not only to themselves but also to others in the classroom.

Tactic: First, base instruction and activities on the premise that tangible rewards together with positive reinforcement can offer real-life relevance and, thus, hold your students' interest and increase their motivation to achieve. Develop a reward system based on a real-life scenario, such as earning coupons by behaving appropriately and redeeming them for library research on an appropriate area of interest or computer time. Set goals and record progress on a chart/graph, together with a daily record of the number of coupons students earn. Finally, to provide ongoing challenges, be prepared to increase expectations and criteria for earning coupons as the student reaches plateaus.

Example: My principal believes that we, as teachers, should understand the curriculum across all the grades in our school. Consequently, over the past 10 years, I've taught at several grade levels. So I've actually modified this tactic a bit to appeal to the various interests of my students, as well as the current hot topics of the day. Thus, over the years, they have earned tokens or coupons that can be exchanged for items donated by parents and local businesses, "free" time to work with a peer on a (preapproved) project; etc. Regardless of the grade level or student interest, I contact the students' parents to obtain their support and, hopefully, implemention at home.

Monica T., teacher

Benefits: Integrating real-life relevance into reward systems

- teaches students to take responsibility for their behavior;
- gives students a sense of control; and
- increases the likelihood of more frequent occurrences of appropriate behavior.

RTI Accommodations/Modifications:

Tiers I, II, & III:

- Integrate and combine individual attention plans;
- create instructional groups that include students who are successful in managing their attention/behavior and those who are less skilled; and/or
- monitor and provide support and correction.

Tiers II & III:

- Monitor more closely/frequently and provide extra praise and corrective feedback when needed;
- modify aims/goals as students achieve milestones;
- teach students to chart their own data; and/or
- provide additional visual and verbal prompts to encourage attention and appropriate behavior.

Literature:

Applebaum, M. (2009). *The one-stop guide to implementing RTI: Academic and behavioral interventions, K–12.* Thousand Oaks, CA: Corwin.

Fachin, K. (1996). Teaching Tommy: A second grader with attention deficit hyperactivity disorder. *Phi Delta Kappan, 77,* 437–441.

Chapter 4: **Prepare for Instruction**

Strategy:	**Handle Disruptions Efficiently**

Learning Difference: Social Behaviors

Tactic Title:	**Daily Behavior Monitoring**

Problem: It disrupts the classroom environment and the academic lesson when teachers have to remind students orally about their expected behavior.

Tactic: First, give the student a Daily Behavior Monitoring worksheet (see page 46) that contains a rating system (e.g., 1 = Did not accomplish, 2 = Accomplished somewhat, 3 = Accomplished completely). Next, talk to the student individually about how specific behavior needs to improve. Then, create at least three behavioral goal statements with the student and agree on a reward for accomplishing these goals. Write these behavioral statements, the reward, and the number of points that the student needs to accumulate to receive the reward on the Behavior Monitoring sheet. Sign the agreement together. Give the student a copy of the sheet every day so as to rate his or her own behavior. Finally, rate the student's behavior on the same sheet, keep track of the points given, and send each day's completed sheet home with the student for a parental signature.

Example: Once my students know that they are accountable and responsible for recording their behavior, they really take ownership, especially if their parents are involved as well. It really doesn't take long to see quite dramatic changes. I know that, at first, they tend to give themselves higher ratings, so I also give extra credit for "agreements" with my ratings.

Julio T., teacher

Benefits: Monitoring student behavior together

- clarifies expectations;
- minimizes disruptions; and
- maximizes student awareness and ongoing monitoring of appropriate behavior.

RTI Accommodations/Modifications:

Tiers I, II, & III:

- Collaborate with other teachers to implement behavior monitoring throughout the day;
- involve parents in rating behavior at home as well as in school;
- gradually phase out the number of ratings; and/or
- shift rewards to those that are more "natural," such as praise.

Literature:

DuPaul, G. J., & Kyle, K. E. (1996). Classroom strategies for managing students with ADHD. *Intervention in School and Clinic, 32,* 318–319.

Mooney, P., Ryan, J. B., Uhing, B. M., Reid, R., & Epstein, M. H. (2005). A review of self-management interventions targeting academic outcomes for students with emotional and behavioral disorders. *Journal of Behavior Education, 14,* 203–221.

Reid, R., Trout, A. L., & Shartz, M. (2005). Self-regulation interventions for children with attention deficit/hyperactivity disorder. *Exceptional Children, 71,* 361–377.

Rief, S. F. (1993). *How to reach and teach ADD/ADHD children.* West Nyack, NY: Center for Applied Research in Education.

Daily Behavior Monitoring

Name: _____   **Date:** _____

Behavior: _____

(1) Accomplished

(2) Accomplished Somewhat

(3) Did Not Accomplish

Date	My Rating	Teacher Rating	Parent Rating	Agreements

Chapter 4: **Prepare for Instruction**

Strategy:	**Teach Students to Manage Their Own Behavior**

Learning Difference: Attention; Social Knowledge; Self-control; Social Behaviors; Self-confidence

Tactic Title:	**Point System and Responsibility Log**

Problem: Many students have difficulty with focusing on the task at hand and adhering to classroom rules.

Tactic: Whenever students behave/act appropriately, they receive a point. If the teacher sees inappropriate behavior, a point is removed. Students must acquire a set number of points as the day progresses to attain their "reward" at the end of the day. Give students a small container and a pretermined number of tokens, corn kernals, play pennies, etc. Each time the students demonstrate appropriate behavior for a set time period, they put a chip/token in the container. If students demonstrate inappropriate behavior, a token is removed.

Example: When I first used this tactic, I was the one who was primarily responsible for giving and removing tokens. However, gradually, I taught my students to self-monitor so that they are paying greater attention to their own behavior. I've extended the time periods to the point where some of my students are only reinforcing themselves two or three times per day. Of course, I've had to adjust the rewards as well.

Sebastian S., teacher

Benefits: Monitoring student behavior together

- clarifies expectations;
- minimizes disruptions; and
- maximizes student awareness and ongoing monitoring of appropriate behavior.

RTI Accommodations/Modifications:

Tier I:

- Remind students of expectations for appropriate behavior periodically;
- agree on appropriate and preferred "rewards"; and/or
- teach students to chart their data daily.

Tier II:

- Teach peers to monitor one another's behavior and provide reinforcers (only);
- modify the time periods according to the learning activity; and/or
- provide distraction-free areas for working cooperatively.

Tier III:

- Gradually increase the time period;
- individualize rewards; and/or
- individualize behaviors being monitored.

Literature:

Kerr, M. M., & Nelson, C. M. (2006). *Strategies for managing behavior problems in the classroom* (5th ed.). Upper Saddle River, NH: Merrill/ Prentice Hall.

Konrad, M., Helf, S., & Itoi, M. (2007). More bang for the book: Using children's literature to promote self-determination and literacy skills. *TEACHING Exceptional Children, 40*(1), 64–71.

Murphy, D. M. (1996). Implications of inclusion for general and special education. *The Elementary School Journal, 96*, 469–493.

U. S. Department of Education: Assistance to States for the Education of Children With Disabilities and Preschool Grants for Children with Disabilities; Final Rule. 34 C.F.R. pts. 300–301 (2006).

Use Time Productively

Principle	Strategy
Use Time Productively	Establish Routines and Procedures
	Organize Physical Space
	Allocate Sufficient Time to Academic Activities

Chapter 5: **Use Time Productively**

Strategy:	**Establish Routines and Procedures**

Learning Difference: Attention; Memory (short- and long-term); Social Behaviors

Tactic Title:	**A Time and a Place for Everything**

Problem: Without consistency, many students are less able to focus; consequently, academic time-on-task is reduced.

Tactic: Develop routines and procedures for everyday activities, such as sharpening pencils, entering the classroom, lining up, passing in the hallways, getting a drink, or using the restrooms. (Use the Classroom Routines checklist below) to record your procedures. Take time to teach students how to follow the procedures, step-by-step. Then, reinforce appropriate behavior.

Example: It's really important to take the time at the beginning of the school year to teach procedures step-by-step repeatedly. For example, in our school, when students pass in the hallways, they all walk with their arms folded in front of them and their first finger to their lips (as if making a "sh" sound). So for the first week of school, we practiced everyday; in fact, it was a great way for my students to learn their way around the school. We call it the Lincoln (School) Walk. Incidentally, the custodians love it because students keep their hands off the walls.

Tyra N., teacher

Benefits: Teaching routines and procedures carefully

- reduces interruptions;
- increases instructional time; and
- enhances cooperation among students.

RTI Accommodations/Modifications:

Tier I:

- Praise students publicly for following routines and procedures correctly;
- collaborate with other teachers to develop common routines and procedures; and/or
- provide whole-class incentives for succeeding.

Tier II:

- Provide group incentives/rewards; and/or
- develop specific procedures for working in small groups.

Tier III:

- Break routines and procedures into smaller segments and practice each segment separately; then, when mastered, link segments;
- individualize incentives; and/or
- monitor and provide feedback regularly.

Literature:

Banda, D. R., Grimmett, E., & Hart, S. L. (2009). Activity schedules: Helping students with autism spectrum disorders in general education classrooms manage transition issues. *TEACHING Exceptional Children, 41*(4), 16–21.

Shores, C. (2009). *A comprehensive RTI model: Integrating behavioral and academic interventions.* Thousand Oaks, CA: Corwin.

Simonsen, B., Sugai, G., & Negron, M. (2008). Schoolwide positive behavior supports: Primary systems and practices. *TEACHING Exceptional Children, 40*(6), 32–40.

Classroom Routines

Directions:

Use this worksheet to think through the individual steps of essential classroom/school routines.

Use as many steps as are needed for each routine. Teach each step to your students.

Use the blank spaces to enter routines that are specific to your classroom/teaching situation.

An example is provided.

Routine	Step 1	Step 2	Step 3	Step 4	Step 5
Example: Sharpening pencils	**Walk to the pencil sharpener.**	**Insert your pencil.**	**Press the pencil into the sharpener.**	**Turn the handle and hold pencil as you count to 10. Stop.**	**Quietly return to your seat.**
Using the restroom					
Submitting work					
Gaining teacher attention					
Answering a teacher question in a large-group lesson					
Working on the computer					
Getting a book to read					
Working with a classmate					
Lining up					
Walking in the hallways					
Entering the classroom					
Leaving the classroom					
Storing your materials					
Caring for your materials					
Working independently					
Getting supplies/ materials					
Going on errands					
Entering the building					

Routine	Step 1	Step 2	Step 3	Step 4	Step 5
Running errands to other classrooms, the office, etc.					

Chapter 5: **Use Time Productively**

Strategy:	**Organize Physical Space**

Learning Difference: Mobility; Speaking/Talking; Cognition Mixed; Attention; Social Behaviors; Listening; Seeing; Health

Tactic Title:	**The Power of Organization**

Problem: Teachers often find the physical structure of their classrooms is limiting when they determine the optimal arrangements for instruction and mangagement of student behavior.

Tactic: First, check lesson plans and make sure they are well developed. Make sure there are enough activities in case students finish early. Second, arrange furniture in such a way that students are able to move about the classroom freely, causing minimal distractions. Place easily distracted students in places where little or no interruptions will occur. Third, arrange materials and supplies so that they are readily available to students who need them. Finally, make sure that you are positioned so that you can see all the students. (See Classroom Arrangements, page 56, for basic ways in which classrooms can be organized according to teacher, student, and instructional needs.)

Example: My classroom is very small compared to others. In addition, I have 22 students who present diverse instructional needs, ranging from those with learning and serious emotional disabilities to nonnative English speakers. Of course, the curriculum is grounded in district and state standards; however, I teach through the extensive use of literature and writing. So it is important for my students to be able to work independently, as well as in dyads; we also need to have an area where we can read and discuss as a whole class. I found the secret to be in teaching my students to make transitions from one task/setting to another without delay. I also make sure that all supplies/materials are easily accessible. This way, we do not lose important instruction time.

Caesar F., teacher

Benefits: Organizing the classroom carefully

- provides opportunities for individual, as well as small-group and large-group instruction;
- accommodates coteachers and paraprofessionals; and
- maximizes instructional time and minimizes delays/interruptions due to behavior.

RTI Accommodations/Modifications:

Tiers I & II:

- Create space for whole-class activities;
- teach students routines for transitions; and/or
- ensure visibility for all students.

Tier III:

- Seat individual students with visual, hearing, or attention issues preferentially;
- use microphones or sound systems for students with hearing disabilities; and/or
- keep instructional supplies/materials in the same place.

Literature:

Guernsey, M. A. (1989). Classroom organization: A key to successful management. *Academic Therapy, 25,* 55–58.

Ridling, Z. (1994, April). *The effects of three seating arrangements on teachers' use of selective interactive verbal behaviors.* Paper presented at the annual meeting of the American Educational Research Association, New Orleans, LA.

Salend, S. (2008). *Creating inclusive classrooms: Effective and reflective practices* (6th ed.). Upper Saddle River, NJ: Merrill/Prentice Hall.

Inclusive Classroom Arrangements

Directions: The classroom arrangements depicted below are designed to accommodate diverse learners, coteaching, and varied instructional needs. Use this chart together with Table 2: *Instructional Planning and Learning Phases chart* in the preface to design a classroom arrangement that meets instructional and learning needs. (Dark gray areas indicate: black/white/chalk/smart boards and/or storage for instructional/student materials.)

FLEXIBLE

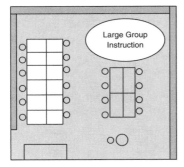

LEARNING CENTERS

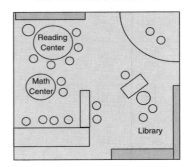

<u>Instruction</u>

Large/Small Group/Individual

Teacher-directed

Peer Interactions

Physical and Content Area Transitions

Easily Accessible Materials and Storage

<u>Instruction</u>

Small Group/Individual Instruction

Teacher- and/or Student-directed

Peer Interactions

Physical and Content Area Transitions

Easily Accessible Materials and Storage

TRADITIONAL

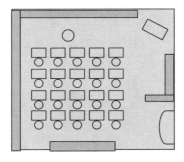

U-SHAPED

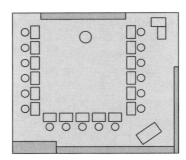

<u>Instruction</u>

Large Group

Teacher-directed

Limited Peer Interactions

Content Area Transitions

Materials Distributed/Student Desks

<u>Instruction</u>

Large Group

Teacher-directed

Limited Peer Interactions

Content Area Transitions

Materials Distributed/Student Desks

Chapter 5: **Use Time Productively**

Strategy:	**Allocate Sufficient Time to Academic Activities**

Learning Difference: Attention; Processing Verbal Information; Gross Motor; Memory Short-term; Fitness

Tactic Title:	**Reducing Transition Time in Physical Education**

Problem: Off-task and inappropriate behavior can be the result of long lines, poor transitions, and a lack of equipment when doing activities.

Tactic: Explain general transition procedures/expectations to students at the beginning of the school year. Define transition time and discuss the negative effects of unnecesary time wasted while moving from one activity to the next. Then, introduce this tactic to the students. To reduce transition time, offer a reward for the students for demonstrating appropriate behavior. This reward is a physical activity reinforcement involving participation in physical activities they enjoy. Set a goal for the time you want the class to move efficiently from one activity to the next. For example, give them 5 minutes to be on the gym floor, then 1 minute to get from warming up into attendance line, then 45 seconds to get from line to learning stations, etc. Offer the students physical activity reinforcement at your own discretion. Chart and post transition time for each class.

Example: This tactic is not difficult to employ, but it did take some preparation and extra motivation on my part. Then, I set aside time for physical activities that students enjoy if they met the criteria for x number of periods/ sessions. In my case, if a student's name appears three times, he or she earns 10 minutes of preferred physical activity.

My transitions were these:

1. Moving from the locker room to the warm-up area 5 minutes after the tardy bell, dressed and in their squad lines

2. Moving from their squad lines to the first instruction site in 40 seconds

I posted student names and times on a bulletin board in the hallway where it was visible to everyone. The effect was immediate and dramatic. Efficient transitions are no longer an issue in my classes.

Jerry R., physical education teacher

Benefits: Developing a management plan to reduce transition time

- increases on-task behavior and academic learning time;
- enhances student motivation to participate; and
- is applicable across grade levels and content areas.

RTI Accommodations/Modifications:

>   *Tier I:*
>
>   - Modify the time criteria for students with special needs, as needed;
>   - adjust times and reinforcers according to student ages; and/or
>   - select reinforcers that focus not only on physical activity but other aspects of health/well-being as well.
>
>   *Tier II:*
>
>   - Organize students into small groups and select the best individual transition time from a group to record; and/or
>   - use group reinforcers.
>
>   *Tier III:*
>
>   - Develop individual criteria and reinforcers to accommodate the needs and abilities of individual students;
>   - praise individual accomplishment publicly; and/or
>   - provide additional visual and auditory cues as reminders.

Literature:

Banda, D. R., Grimmett, E., & Hart, S. L. (2009). Activity schedules: Helping students with autism spectrum disorders in general education classrooms manage transition issues. *TEACHING Exceptional Children, 41*(4), 16–21.

Lacourse, M. (1997). A plan to reduce transition time in physical education. *Journal of Physical Education, Recreation & Dance, 68,* 30.

Lee, D. L. (2006). Facilitating transitions between and within academic tasks. *Remedial and Special Education, 27,* 312–317.

Stecker, P. M., Whinnery, K. Q., & Duxh, L. A. (1996). Self-recording during unsupervised academic activity: Effects on time spent out of class. *Exceptionality, 6,* 133–147.

6

Establish
Positive Environments

Principle	Strategy
Establish Positive Environments	Make the Classroom a Pleasant, Friendly Place
	Accept Individual Differences
	Establish Supportive, Cooperative Learning Environments
	Create a Nonthreatening Learning Environment

Chapter 6: **Establish Positive Environments**

Strategy:	**Make the Classroom a Pleasant, Friendly Place**

Learning Difference: Attention; Social Competence; Self-efficacy; Self-confidence

Tactic Title:	**Keeping an Open Door**

Problem: Classrooms need to be special places where students and others feel welcome and safe.

Tactic: Open your classroom door. Post your typical daily schedule outside the door so visitors know where you are if you are not in the classroom. Make sure there are places for visitors to sit without being disruptive if you and your students are actively engaged in a focused activity. Encourage visitors to participate and engage when appropriate. Teach your students how to react to visitors: ignoring is acceptable sometimes; sharing learning objectives and current activities is acceptable at other times.

Example: My students are an amazing group of individual learners. They represent at least seven cultures and three languages. They enrich my life, both personally and professionally. Because each child is so distinctive, we work continuously on ways to create a common community of learners. I also wanted to enrich our classroom by encouraging others to share time with us. So our classroom door is *always* open. People know they are welcome to visit at any time. On any given day, a student from the university might videotape for an hour or two for her research, the learning specialist/paraprofessional might work with one or two students on a math skill for 30 minutes, the writing specialist might coteach a lesson with me, my principal might observe, the assistant superintent might drop by, or a parent might show up to volunteer. Some of it is planned; however, a lot is not. So we can still complete the day's work, I've taught my students to be welcoming yet continue to focus on their learning. It's getting close to the end of the school year, and I would say that not only do my students feel welcome and safe, but they've learned how to welcome others. In doing so, they've distinguished themselves academically as well.

Ruth D., teacher

Keeping your classroom door open

- increases opportunities for additional enrichment from others;
- teaches everyone to accept and welcome new ideas; and
- enhances appropriate attitudes and teaches skills that all individuals need in our diverse society.

RTI Accommodations/Modifications:

Tier I:

- Select one student (on a rotating basis) to be the "Greeter";
- close your door and post a sign when testing or at other times when the presence of visitors would be disruptive; and/or
- use gestures or verbal cues to let visitors know what to do; some will not need them after time.

Tier II:

- Pair students with socially and/or academically skilled partners who can model appropriate behavior;
- use preferential seating; and/or
- create group reward systems for reinforcing appropriate welcoming behaviors.

Tier III:

- Model appropriate social behaviors;
- teach students how to make wise choices to develop social competence; and/or
- praise individual accomplishments publicly.

Literature:

Campbell, P., & Siperstein, G. P. (1994). *Developing social competence: A resource for elementary teachers.* Boston: Allyn & Bacon.

CEC's policy on safe and positive school climate. (2008). *TEACHING Exceptional Children, 40*(6), 41–42.

Pearl, C. (2009). Laying the foundation for self-advocacy: Fourth graders with learning disabilities invite their peers into the resource room. *TEACHING Exceptional Children, 36*(3), 44–49.

Wang, M. C., Haertel, G. D., & Walberg, H. J. (1993). Toward a knowledge base for school learning. *Review of Educational Research, 63,* 249–294.

Chapter 6: **Establish Positive Environments**

Strategy:	**Accept Individual Differences**

Learning Difference: Social Knowledge; Speaking/Talking

Tactic Title:	**Bridging the Bilingual Divide Through Literature Circles**

Problem: Although ESL instruction can enable students who are bilingual to overcome language barriers, many educators do not know how to address the cultural divide created in the classroom that can disrupt the flow of student learning.

Tactic: First, read a story that either incorporates a different culture into its theme or specifically uses different languages in its text. Then, divide students into literature groups of four or five, preferably with at least one student with a different cultural experience in each group. Groups then reread the story together and discuss guiding questions related to the story. Guiding questions may include what they liked or didn't like, what they related to and why, and if they have had experiences similar to those of the characters in the story. Then, bring students back together as a whole group to reflect and share their experiences. Encourage students to talk about cultural differences they found in the text and the ways in which their group conversations involved these differences. Summarize the activity, reflections, and common learning experiences. Use this information to plan subsequent activities/lessons.

Example: Literature is a wonderful tool to teach students about other cultures, as well as the day-to-day lives of individuals in their community. I found several books this year that dealt with children and families who were homeless. Together with our writing specialist, we developed an instructional unit based on homelessness, service to the community, and writing. After reading the stories, we all decided on a project: making scarves and blankets to be distributed to homeless people in our neighborhood. Students wrote letters to our building principal and others requesting permission to raise funds by selling bottles of water to pay for material for the scarves and blankets. They subsequently wrote thank-you notes. They also kept individual journals of activities and their reflections. We sold water, raised money, and purchased material (with a generous discount from a local store). Then, we made the scarves and blankets and contacted a local agency to distribute them for us. Finally, we created a book that we've published. A great project that crossed a potential "divide" among my very diverse group of learners!

Paula L., teacher

Benefits: Using literature in creative ways

- fosters academic and social belonging for ESL students;
- creates meaningful learning experiences; and

- reduces miscommunication, increases understanding, and creates an atmosphere of understanding and acceptance among everyone.

RTI Accommodations/Modifications:

    Tier I:

- Provide advanced organizers;
- integrate homework assignments that could interest and involve parents; and/or
- advertise projects to solicit wider involvement.

    Tier II:

- Pair students as reading buddies;
- modify assignments; and/or
- allow extra time to complete assignments.

    Tier III:

- Provide taped versions of the literature;
- preteach vocabulary; and/or
- let students tape their journal entries/reflections.

Literature:

Brown, J. E., & Doolittle, J. (2008). A cultural, linguistic, and ecological framework for response to intervention with English language learners. *TEACHING Exceptional Children, 40*(5), 66–72.

Martinez-Roldan, C. M., & Lopez-Robertson, J. M. (2000). Initiating literature circles in a first-grade bilingual classroom. *The Reading Teacher, 53,* 270–281.

Chapter 6: Establish Positive Environments

Strategy:	**Establish Supportive, Cooperative Learning Environments**

Learning Difference: Social Behaviors; Self-control; Attention

Tactic Title:	**Creating a System to Support Appropriate Student Behavior**

Problem: Many students struggle with maintaining appropriate behavior across time and locations.

Tactic: First, establish and teach rules and procedures for your classroom. Meanwhile, collaborate with other teachers/educators who share responsibility for your students. Focus on the concept of self-discipline rather than punishment. Work in teams to develop a common rubric of appropriate actions and behaviors, goals and objectives, as well as a common code of conduct. When the students see their actions as affecting an entire community, they are often more likely to internalize proper behavior and self-discipline.

Example: In my school, we did it in reverse. First, we developed a system of behavior management that everyone uses—the principal, office staff, teachers, custodians, and visitors. We share and implement the same expectations, rules and procedures, and consequences. Of course, we have rules and procedures that are specific to our individual classrooms and settings; however, in the common areas (hallways, cafeteria, playground, etc.), we are all on the same page. Then, using the schoolwide rubric/criteria, we determined our individual classroom rules and procedures. Seems to be working very well . . . clarifying and simplifying expectations for students and reducing behavioral issues.

Eduardo F., teacher

Benefits: Using a common schoolwide system to support students

- creates a sense of continuity for students;
- models cooperative planning and implementation; and
- reduces potential misunderstandings/misinterpretations among students and teachers.

RTI Accommodations/Modifications:

Tier I:

- Use the schoolwide model as the basis for your classroom rules/procedures;
- teach students the value and importance of rules/procedures in creating a supportive, cooperative learning environment; and/or
- provide opportunities for practice.

Tier II:

- Reinforce smaller groups of students for appropriate behavior;
- post cues and reminders; and/or
- develop special rules for small groups.

Tier III:

- Develop rules/procedures that are specific to the needs and abilities of individual students;
- implement individualized systems for the management of behavior; and/or
- select students who are skilled in terms of adhering to the rules to serve as peer buddies for students who are less skilled.

Literature:

Din, F. S., Isack, L. R., & Rietveld, J. (2003, February–March). *Effects of contingency contracting on decreasing student tardiness.* Paper presented at the annual conference of the Eastern Educational Research Association, Hilton Head Island, SC.

Lassen, S. R., Steele, M. M., & Sailor, W. (2006). The relationship of school-wide positive behavior support to academic achievement in an urban middle school. *Psychology in the School, 43,* 701–712.

Oswald, K., Safran, S., & Johanson, G. (2005). Preventing trouble: Making schools safer places using positive behavior supports. *Education and Treatment of Children, 28,* 265–278.

Rosenberg, M. S., & Jackman, L. A. (2003). Development, implementation, and sustainability of comprehensive schoolwide behavior management systems. *Intervention in School and Clinic, 39,* 10–21.

Simonsen, B., Sugai, G., & Negron, M. (2008). Schoolwide positive behavior supports: Primary systems and practices. *TEACHING Exceptional Children, 40*(6), 32–40.

Wilkinson, L. A. (2003). Using behavioral consultation to reduce challenging behavior in the classroom. *Preventing School Failure, 47*(3), 100–105.

Chapter 6: **Establish Positive Environments**

| *Strategy:* | **Create a Nonthreatening Learning Environment** |

Learning Difference: Social Knowledge

| *Tactic Title:* | **Creating a Safe and Welcoming Classroom** |

Problem: Determining how to make students with diverse learning needs feel welcome in your classroom is often challenging.

Tactic: First, discuss the need to accept diverse learners and learning styles, including those who might be particularly challenging (e.g., students who throw tantrums, exhibit selective mutism, withdraw, etc.). Next, select several students to partner with others in completing classroom assignments, organizing materials, and negotiating social interactions. Find ways (see RTI Accommodations/Modifications: Tier I below) to incorporate all students into activities without overwhelming them.

Example: I remember that several years ago, we learned that a student with spina bifida would be joining our class in January. Not knowing that much about spina bifida, I talked with our school nurse and our special education team to learn as much as I could. They were very helpful—gave me lots of resources, including the Web sites of the Spina Bifida Association (www.spinabifidaassociation.org) and the Council for Exceptional Children (www.cec.sped.org), just for starters. Then, I also knew that I had to prepare my students for this new member of our classroom community. I brought lots of resources into the classroom: the mother and father of the student to share how special their daughter was, the school nurse to talk about wheelchairs and leg braces and give each student an opportunity to practice moving around the classroom and the school using them, and the daughter of one of our teachers who've been living with spina bifida for the last 20 years. When Camilla finally arrived, she found a safe, nonthreatening learning environment waiting for her. The other students couldn't wait to meet her and include her in our classroom community.

Marina H., teacher

Benefits: Taking the time to create a safe and welcoming classroom

- provides new students with a sense of safety;
- gives classmates a sense of importance and ownership; and
- reduces potential behavioral problems or misunderstandings.

RTI Accommodations/Modifications:

Tier I:

- Consider the physical arrangement of your classroom; and/or
- ensure that all students have access to all aspects of instruction.

Tier II:

- Pair students with supportive partners; and/or
- modify materials to enable students to meet instructional goals/objectives.

Tier III:

- Increase opportunities for active engagement; and/or
- provide ongoing monitoring, feedback, and support.

Literature:

McNeely, C. A., Nonnemaker, J. M., & Blum, R. W. (2002). Promoting school connectedness: Evidence from the National Longitudinal Study of Adolescent Health. *Journal of School Health, 72*(4), 138–146.

National Institute of Child Health and Human Development Early Child Care Research Network. (2005). A day in third grade: A large-scale study of classroom quality and teacher and student behavior. *Elementary School Journal, 105*, 305–323.

Swinson, J., & Knight, R. (2007). Teacher verbal feedback directed towards secondary pupils with challenging behaviour and its relationship to their behaviour. *Educational Psychology in Practice, 23*, 241–255.

PART III

Delivering Instruction

Teaching is systematic presentation of content. Effective teachers present information in carefully monitored lessons, which they adjust to meet the needs of their students. In this part of our resource, we describe evidence-based strategies for each principle of delivering instruction.

Component	Principle	Strategy
Delivering Instruction (Part III)	Present Information (Chapter 7)	*Presenting Content*
		Gain and Maintain Attention
		Review Prior Skills or Lessons
		Provide Organized, Relevant Lessons
		Motivating Students
		Show Enthusiasm and Interest
		Use Rewards Effectively
		Consider Level and Student Interest
		Teaching Thinking Skills
		Model Thinking Skills
		Teach Fact-Finding Skills
		Teach Divergent Thinking
		Teach Learning Strategies
		Providing Relevant Practice
		Develop Automaticity
		Vary Opportunities for Practice/Vary Methods of Practice
		Monitor Amount of Work Assigned

(Continued)

(Continued)

Component	Principle	Strategy
	Monitor Presentations (Chapter 8)	*Providing Feedback*
		Give Immediate, Frequent, Explicit Feedback/ Provide Specific Praise and Encouragement
		Model Correct Performance
		Provide Prompts and Cues
		Check Student Understanding
		Keeping Students Actively Involved
		Monitor Performance Regularly/Monitor Performance During Practice
		Use Peers to Improve Instruction
		Provide Opportunities for Success/Limit Opportunities for Failure
		Monitor Engagement Rates
	Adjust Presentations (Chapter 9)	Adapt Lessons to Meet Student Needs
		Provide Varied Instructional Options
		Alter Pace

Delivering Instruction Works: A Case Study

When working with diverse learners in an inclusive setting, teachers must draw upon a variety of delivery methods. I teach in an English language arts classroom with a writing-based curriculum. The challenge is how to teach the diversity of learning styles across Tiers I, II, and III. In addition, many of my students have disabilities in writing or reading and need assistance with classroom tasks such as note taking. I assign students a note buddy who helps them read and take notes. Students in my classroom are seated at tables and sit in mixed-ability groups. This allows them to help each other and doesn't draw attention to students with lower abilities. Some of the students I teach need to have preferential seating. All students are assigned seats at the beginning of the year, allowing the accommodation of those needing to be seated up front. I am able to monitor work as the students progress.

Vocabulary is especially challenging to teach, but with the use of "foldables" that incorporate both pictures and words, students with problems in reading have visual cues to help them understand the meaning of words. I adjust the specific words, as well as the number of words, according to whether a student needs Tier I, II, or III instruction. Students work together to help each other study orally for tests. This again addresses the diversity of learning styles found within an inclusive classroom.

Likewise, when working on a writing assignment, students are able to collaborate on assignments and work in edit groups to aid those with lower writing abilities. We work individually and do "group writes" to accommodate the diversity of ability levels in the class. This allows all students the opportunity to succeed.

—Rene Segler
Middle School English Teacher

7

Present Information

Component	Principle	Strategy
Delivering Instruction	Present Information	*Presenting Content*
		Gain and Maintain Attention
		Review Prior Skills or Lessons
		Provide Organized, Relevant Lessons
		Motivating Students
		Show Enthusiasm and Interest
		Use Rewards Effectively
		Consider Level and Student Interest
		Teaching Thinking Skills
		Model Thinking Skills
		Teach Fact-Finding Skills
		Teach Divergent Thinking
		Teach Learning Strategies
		Providing Relevant Practice
		Develop Automaticity
		Vary Opportunities for Practice/Vary Methods of Practice
		Monitor Amount of Work Assigned

Chapter 7: **Present Information**

Strategy:	**Gain and Maintain Attention**

Learning Difference: Attention; Self-control; Social Behaviors

Tactic Title:	**Using Eye Contact and Physical Proximity Effectively**

Problem: Some students need extra support and time in order to focus on a lesson.

Tactic: First, make direct start requests, such as "Please take out your writing journals." Second, move closer, while making eye contact, to students who are having difficulty settling down. Third, if students do not comply, make the request again. Fourth, give students an appropriate amount of time to respond. Finally, praise students for following directions and tell them how complying will help them learn more successfully.

Example: Most of my students follow directions pretty well. However, it is essential to have everyone's attention before beginning a lesson. Sometimes, I use Take Five, where I say, "Take five," and hold up five fingers. Students stop what they are doing, hold up five fingers, and look at me. I also use Take Five at other points in a lesson or other times during the school day if we need to stop and regroup before continuing with an activity. Everyone in our school uses Take Five, so there is consistency for the students across classrooms and grades. I've seen teachers in the younger grades also put their index finger to their lips to indicate the need to be quiet.

Thalia R., teacher

Benefits: Gaining and maintaining student attention

- teaches students to be responsible for their own actions and behaviors;
- increases the likelihood of their remaining on-task and following directions; and
- emphasizes appropriate cooperative behavior.

RTI Accommodations/Modifications:

Tier I:

- State directions in very simple terms;
- provide visual cues, in addition to verbal instructions; and/or
- praise students publicly to enhance perception of their responses as appropriate.

Tiers II & III:

- Modify directions to meet special physical arrangements;
- pair students with a partner who follows instructions well; and/or
- monitor and record appropriate responding and reward appropriately.

Literature:

Foster, K. C. (2008). The transformative potential of teacher care as described by students in a higher education access initiative. *Education and Urban Society, 41*(1), 104–126.

Gable, R. A., Hester, P. H., Rock, M. L., & Hughes, K. G. (2009). Back to basics: Rules, praise, ignoring, and reprimands revisited. *Intervention in School and Clinic, 44,* 195–205.

Miller, S. P. (2009). *Validated practices for teaching students with diverse needs and abilities* (2nd ed.). Upper Saddle River, NJ: Pearson/Merrill.

Noddings, N. (2005). *The challenge to care in schools: An alternative approach to education* (2nd ed.). New York: Teachers College Press.

Chapter 7: **Present Information**

Strategy:	**Review Prior Skills or Lessons**

Learning Difference: Cognition Low; Attention; Memory Long-term

Tactic Title:	**"Jeopardy" Game Math Review**

Problem: Frequently students—particularly those with attention difficulties—lose interest quickly when asked to perform repetitive exercises like those often used to review basic math concepts.

Tactic: Following a *Jeopardy!* game model, the instructor prepares a board with five vertical columns (numbered 1 through 5) consisting of five envelopes per column. In each column, the five envelopes are assigned (and labeled with) point values from 10 to 50 in ascending order (i.e., the top envelope is worth 10 points, the next 20, and so on). The envelopes each contain a math problem "worthy" of the point value assigned—the more difficult the problem, the more points it is worth. The instructor acts as the game show host, calling on every student—in order of seating—so that every student has the same number of turns to select a question and earn points.

Example: I used *Jeopardy!* to review Roman numerals. Each envelope contained a card with either a number to be converted into a Roman numeral or vice versa. In turn, students came to the whiteboard to write (if physically able) their answers. There was no penalty incurred for incorrect answers, only credit received for supplying correct answers. The points earned by the students could be "spent" on a particular classroom privilege—using the computer (for instructional purposes), working with a peer, silent reading, etc. I added the extra incentive of a special activity if the class as a whole earned a specific total number of points.

Kelly R., teacher

Benefits: Using game formats for review

- helps to generate interest in, and sustain the attention of, easily distractible students;
- can be used across content areas and grade levels; and
- fosters both individual and cooperative learning.

RTI Accommodations/Modifications:

Tier I:

- Modify content to match current learning goals/objectives;
- provide easy access to game for all students; and/or
- remove distractors.

Tier II:

- Match student ability levels with question difficulty;
- have students work in pairs; and/or
- adjust time intervals.

Tier III:

- Provide visual or auditory cues;
- extend response time; and/or
- modify types of responses to increase student success.

Literature:

Bender, W. N. (2009). *Differentiating math instruction: Strategies that work for K–8 classrooms* (2nd ed.). Thousand Oaks, CA: Corwin.

Jitendra, A. K., Deatline-Buchman, A., & Sczesniak, E. (2005). A comparative analysis of third-grade mathematics textbooks before and after the 2000 NCTM standards. *Effective Intervention, 30,* 47–62.

Lance, D. M., Beverly, B. L., Evans, L. H., & McCullough, K. C. (2003). Addressing literacy: Effective methods for reading instruction. *Communication Disorders Quarterly, 25,* 5–11.

Miller, S. P. (2009). *Validated practices for teaching students with diverse needs and abilities* (2nd ed.). Upper Saddle River, NJ: Pearson/Merrill.

Chapter 7: **Present Information**

Strategy:	**Provide Organized, Relevant Lessons**

Learning Difference: Cognition Mixed; Attention; Study Skills; Memory Short-term; Memory Long-term

Tactic Title:	**An Organizational Model for Planning Instruction**

Problem: Oftentimes it is poor instructional planning that hinders learning, especially for children with learning disabilities.

Tactic: When combined with peer tutoring, the following model for instructional planning has been shown to increase academic achievement.

1. Review prerequisite skills.

2. Give the specifications and purposes of the lesson objective.

3. Model multiple examples.

4. Give adequate guided practice.

5. Give appropriate, corrective feedback.

6. Prepare students for independent practice.

7. Monitor independent practice.

Providing this framework helps put learning in context for students. It also helps them organize their learning experiences, because they are told specifically what will be taking place and why the content is important to learn.

Example: I try to be consistent in my presentation of lessons. Reviewing prerequisite skills is important for everyone; however, it is absolutely essential for my students with special learning needs. They also have much greater success when they are paired with another student who is more skilled with the learning objective. It's important to teach students how to tutor, to monitor the tutoring, and to praise effective tutoring. While this does take additional time at first, peer tutoring has been demonstrated to be effective both for the tutee and the tutor.

Camilla R., teacher

Benefits: Providing an organizational framework for students

- provides consistency across lessons;
- can be combined with peer tutoring for greater effectiveness; and
- is supported by evidence in the literature.

RTI Accommodations/Modifications:

> *Tier I:*
>
> - Differentiate instruction according to student abilities and needs;
> - pair students with skilled learners as models and tutors; and/or
> - modify individual amounts of guided practice.
>
> *Tier II:*
>
> - Preteach or review prerequisite skills needed for subsequent large-group lessons/activities;
> - provide visual cues to remind students of assigned tasks; and/or
> - provide alternative response modes.
>
> *Tier III:*
>
> - Limit steps in instruction;
> - provide individual cue cards or outlines; and/or
> - monitor performance closely.

Literature:

Hurd, D. W. (1997). Novelty and its relation to field trips. *Education/Print Source Plus, 118,* 29–35.

Schumm, J. S., Vaughn, S., Haager, D., McDowell, J., Rothlein, L., & Saumell, L. (1995). General education teacher planning: What can students with learning disabilities expect? *Exceptional Children, 61,* 335–352.

Schumm, J. S., Vaughn, S., & Leavell, A. G. (1994). Planning pyramid: A framework for planning for diverse student needs during content area instruction. *The Reading Teacher, 47,* 608–615.

Simmons, D., Fuchs, D., & Fuchs, L. (1991). Instructional and curricular requisites of mainstreamed students with learning disabilities. *Journal of Learning Disabilities, 24,* 354–360.

Chapter 7: **Present Information**

Strategy:	**Show Enthusiasm and Interest**

Learning Difference: Attention; Speaking/Talking

Tactic Title:	**Maintaining Attention in the Classroom**

Problem: Frequently, students who are second-language learners have a tendency to lose their focus on classroom activities; consequently, they fall behind and lose interest as well.

Tactic: First, try to be more energetic to capture the students' attention. Often they will imitate your behavior. Next, incorporate visual and auditory representations/cues so that students can use more than a single modality in gaining understanding. Finally, if students still seem to lack interest, seat them in the "action zone," where they are more apt to participate. Keep the lessons focused on the students' level of interest and incorporate "authentic activities" to which they can relate in real-life situations.

Example: I remember, when I was student teaching many years ago, my cooperating teacher used to do the craziest things to catch her students off guard and capture their attention. For example, she came to school wearing a red shoe and a blue shoe. Once, in the middle of a lesson, she took off her glasses, flipped her hair right over her face, put her glasses back on and kept right on teaching. Didn't miss a beat. I learned very quickly that her tactics worked! Her students were interested, they were involved, and they were learning. Now I have my own bag of tricks.

Shelley L., teacher

Benefits: Showing enthusiasm and interest

- models desired attitudes and behaviors for students;
- results in greater student participation; and
- demonstrates concern and caring behavior.

RTI Accommodations/Modifications:

Tier I:

- Use peers as tutors;
- supplement instruction with appropriate computer activities or taped books; and/or
- involve others (educators and parents) in brainstorming appropriate topics and activities.

Tier II:

- Preteach or review English sentence structures;
- teach and reteach essential vocabulary; and/or
- provide alternative response modes to encourage use of English.

Tier III:

- Modify the number of new vocabulary words presented;
- increase opportunities for guided practice; and/or
- remember to ask the student(s) to clarify interests, misunderstandings, etc.

Literature:

Mastropieri, M. A., Scruggs, T. E., & Bohs, K. (1994). Mainstreaming an emotionally handicapped student in science: A qualitative investigation. In T. E. Scruggs & M. A. Mastropieri (Eds.), *Advances in learning and behavioral disabilities* (Vol. 8; pp. 131–146). Greenwich, CT: JAI.

Mastropieri, M. A., Scruggs, T. E., & Cicciarelli, S. (2007, April). *Overcoming a significant challenge: Motivating students to learn!* Paper presented at the annual meeting of the Council for Exceptional Children, Louisville, KY.

Parris, S. R., & Block, C. C. (2007). The expertise of adolescent literacy teachers. *Journal of Adolescent & Adult Literacy, 50,* 582–596.

Chapter 7: **Present Information**

Strategy:	**Use Rewards Effectively**

Learning Difference: Cognition Mixed; Attention

Tactic Title:	**Timeless Review and Practice**

Problem: Many students with learning differences become anxious and frustrated during mathematics instruction. Consequently, their commitment to task completion is limited.

Tactic: Using everyday game boards, where players advance based on points earned, is an effective way to use the Timeless Review and Practice tool. First, determine an appropriate reward for completing the game. Then, make categories of mathematics problems or math facts (e.g., addition, subtraction, etc.) that are appropriate for the skill levels of your students. Make problems for each category and set a score standard. For example, make easier problems worth 2 points and more difficult problems worth 5 points. Use different colored cards for each category. Give students individual game boards and a chip or marker to use to advance on the game board. Then, tell students to choose a category and complete a problem in that category, with no time limit. Verify their answers and award the corresponding number of points so they can move their marker. Continue the game either until one student "wins" by progressing through all of the spaces on the board or until the end of the instructional period. Play until the students reach their goal. Give the reward to the winners. Then congratulate all students on their efforts and accomplishments.

Example: Games that incorporate rewards are a wonderful way to heighten student interest and engage students in learning activities. I remember a wonderful book by Marge Golick (1985) in which she showed how to use ordinary playing cards to teach all kinds of mathematics and language skills. I used small plastic bags that contained a deck of cards and simple directions as to how to play the game inside (title of game, number of players, learning objective, directions, reward). I've used them in learning centers, as well as "free time" activities. I simply tacked the bags to a bulletin board or hung them (like my tape-books) on a "clothesline" in the classroom library.

Rujula G., teacher

Benefits: Using games with rewards

- enables students to persist and focus on tasks because the learning is fun;
- can be modified in terms of content, difficulty, and grade level; and
- provides students with a goal.

RTI Accommodations/Modifications:

> *Tier I:*
>
> - Play the game as a whole group with one winner and one reward;
> - use rewards that reinforce learning; and/or
> - monitor participation of all players.
>
> *Tier II:*
>
> - Divide students into teams or pairs to play the game with multiple winners and rewards;
> - provide additional prompts and cues; and/or
> - use higher points and/or fewer cards to shorten the game.
>
> *Tier III:*
>
> - Develop categories and sets of cards that are specific to individual students;
> - provide a reward that is specific to one student; and/or
> - extend the playing time across class sessions.

Literature:

Akande, A. (1997). The role of reinforcement in self-monitoring. *Education, 118,* 275.

Bender, W. N. (2009). *Differentiating math instruction: Strategies that work for K–8 classrooms* (2nd ed.). Thousand Oaks, CA: Corwin.

Golick, M. (1985). *Deal me in.* New York: Norton.

Peterson-Miller, S. (1996). Promoting strategic math performance to students with learning disabilities. *Learning Disabilities Forum, 21,* 34–40.

Chapter 7: **Present Information**

Strategy:	**Consider Level and Student Interest**

Learning Difference: Cognition High

Tactic Title:	**Engaging Students With Gifts and Talents**

Problem: Students with gifts and talents are often bored with the traditional curriculum, especially with repeated review.

Tactic: First, brainstorm with students who are gifted to find a topic within the basic curriculum that interests them. For example, if your class will be reading a story about (or studying) animals, perhaps a small group of students with gifts and talents might want to investigate endangered species or animals of the rain forest. Provide a timeline for their project; any components, such as a presentation to the other students; and grading criteria. Next, let these students use in-class or library resources, including the Internet, books, other teachers, and community resources. After students finish gathering information, they finalize their project and schedule a day and time to share their learning with the rest of the class. They might, for example, present a mock news report to inform their peers about the dangers of environmental abuse and/or hunting.

Example: Last spring, I was teaching my sixth-grade students about bar graphs, and since I always preassess my students, I realized that several of them were already proficient in using bar graphs. At the same time, there happened to be a food drive underway at our school. So the students and I developed a plan to categorize and track food drive items as they were collected. They chose how they would do this, and they could incorporate as many different graphs as they wanted. We developed a rubric together that would let us know that they had mastered the material. Then, they presented their findings to the eighth-grade Service Learning Leaders, who had sponsored the project. My students used PowerPoint, cameras (to take pictures), and a variety of graphs to represent their data. They were able to take an academic topic for which they had prerequisite knowledge and explore it in even greater depth and using a real-life experience. My students enjoyed the challenge and were very successful. The eighth graders used the documentation to back up their future desire to have another food drive.

Shannon H., teacher

Benefits: Providing enrichment learning opportunities for students with gifts and talents

- enables students to remain participants in class activities while providing additional resources and information to their classmates;
- enables them to use their individual gifts and talents to explore areas of special interest; and
- ensures their ongoing participation and contributions.

RTI Accommodations/Modifications:

> *Tier I:*
>
> - Differentiate learning outcomes, response modes, and evaluative criteria for students with gifts and talents;
> - assign leadership roles to students with gifts and talents; and/or
> - assign greater responsibilities as students are able to accept them.
>
> *Tier II:*
>
> - Divide students into teams or pairs to conduct research;
> - schedule time for small-group work;
> - teach students ways to self-monitor their progress; and/or
> - develop rules and procedures that are specific to small groups or dyads.
>
> *Tier III:*
>
> - Permit students to work independently on projects;
> - minimize content review for skill already mastered, while maintaining and generalizing learned material; and/or
> - raise academic expectations while maintaining expectations for appropriate behavior.

Literature:

Cunningham, M., Corprew III, C. S., & Becker, J. E. (2009). Associations of future expectations, negative friends, and academic achievement in high-achieving African American adolescents. *Urban Education, 44,* 280–296.

Gentry, M., Hu, S., Peters, S. J., & Rizza, M. (2008). Talented students in an exemplary career and technical education school: A qualitative inquiry. *Gifted Child Quarterly, 52,* 183–198.

Hall, S. L. (2008). *Implementing response to intervention.* Thousand Oaks, CA: Corwin.

Joseph, L. M., & Konrad, M. (2009). Have students self-manage their academic performance. *Intervention in School and Clinic, 44,* 246–249.

Lee, S.-H., Palmer, S. B., & Wehmeyer, M. L. (2009). Goal setting and self-monitoring for students with disabilities: Practical tips and ideas for teachers. *Intervention in School and Clinic, 44,* 139–145.

Renzulli, J. S., & Reis, S. M. (2002). What is schoolwide enrichment and how do gifted programs relate to total school improvement? *Gifted Child Today, 25*(4), 18–25.

Chapter 7: **Present Information**

Strategy:	**Model Thinking Skills**

Learning Difference: Study Skills; Cognition Mixed; Self-confidence; Receptive Language/Decoding (listening, reading)

Tactic Title:	**Teaching Students to Monitor Their Own Learning**

Problem: Students frequently lack metacognitive learning strategies and, therefore, do poorly on their learning tasks.

Tactic: Before letting students begin a task, model the learning processes to be used during the task for students. Present each step of self-monitoring in sequence. Provide a list of questions for students to ask themselves (a) before performing a task, (b) during performance of the task, and (c) after completing the task. For example, you might ask the following:

Before Beginning: What is my learning objective? What materials do I need? Do I know what to do? Do I know how to complete the task? When do I need to be finished?

During the Task: Am I making progress? Do I need assistance? How do I get my teacher's attention?

After the Task: Where do I put my completed work? What am I supposed to do if I finish early? What have I learned? What do I still want to know? How can I find the answers?

As you model each step of the task, ask yourself the questions and then answer them aloud. Repeat the process; however, this time, ask the questions in sequence and have the students supply the answers. Talk through the processes that are used during the task, offering assistance as needed. Repeat the process for each subsequent assignment given to the students; however, modify the amount of assistance provided as students become more skilled at self-monitoring their learning.

Example: I know that when I study for a test, I automatically use a variety of tricks to enable me to recall information. Sometimes, I make up a silly sentence where the first letter of each word is a cue for a term to remember; similarly, I put terms in alphabetical order and then memorize the list of first letters. At other times, because I have a pretty good visual memory, I compress information and put as much as I can on a single page and then memorize how that page looks. This tactic works really well with mathematical/statistical formulas that I had to remember and apply during an exam. Finally, color-coding and highlighting are very effective. I've tried teaching some of my study tactics to my students and find that some work for some students sometimes. So I'm always looking for new ideas. I try not to forget to ask them what works for them, because sometimes they are the experts and have great tactics that we can share with others.

Caleb W., teacher

Benefits: When students use metacognitive learning strategies to self-monitor their own learning, they

- eventually internalize the self-monitoring practice through repeated practice;
- feel more self-confident about their ability to learn; and
- develop a more positive self-image.

RTI Accommodations/Modifications:

Tier I:

- Post the questions and the correct answers where they are clearly visible to all students;
- develop and post acronyms that would help students remember strategies; and/or
- use the strategy repeatedly—across content areas, classes, and tasks—to give students additional practice.

Tier II:

- Monitor student use of the tactic;
- organize students into small groups or dyads to enable them to remind one another of the tactic; and/or
- use graphic organizers, such as outlines or syllabi.

Tier III:

- Provide individual cue cards to post on student desks;
- ask a student to repeat the steps to you individually; and/or
- adjust the number of components/questions according to individual student abilities and needs.

Literature: Kucan, L., & Beck, I. L. (1997). Thinking aloud and reading comprehension research: Inquiry, instruction, and social interaction. *Review of Educational Research, 67,* 271–299.

Schlichter, C. L. (1986). An inservice education model for teaching thinking skills. *Gifted Child Quarterly, 30,* 119–123.

Vaidya, S. R. (1999). Metacognitive learning strategies for students with learning disabilities. *Education, 120,* 186–189.

Chapter 7: **Present Information**

Strategy:	**Teach Fact-Finding Skills**

Learning Difference: Speaking/Talking; Hearing; Processing Visual Information; Receptive Language/Decoding (listening, reading); Expressive Language/Encoding (speaking, writing, spelling)

Tactic Title:	**Breaking Down Classroom Content Through Idea Maps**

Problem: Many students, especially those with hearing impairments and/or auditory-processing deficits, have difficulty comprehending expository text, since they cannot hear the language and/or often fail to understand its subtleties.

Tactic: To use idea maps, identify each of the various concepts and terms in the text that students need to learn. Develop a set of guiding questions to help students focus on terms/concepts in the text as they highlight them. While reading the text, they should begin to place their answers on a map created specifically for that text structure by the teacher (e.g., write the theme of the passage in the middle box/circle, with the various concepts of the theme in the boxes branching off of the center box/circle). (Use the Idea Map worksheet on page 88.) After the students have created their maps, they have a visual representation of the information presented in the text, as well as an initial framework for text understanding. These finished idea maps can promote classroom discussion, initiate additional questions on the text, and be used as a self-generated framework for writing organization.

Example: Teaching students how to "map" their thinking is a wonderful instructional tool, and I've used it for several years. As my students' skill in using them has improved, their maps have become more complex; we've even integrated the tactic into other content areas, such as math and science. Idea maps are a tool that assists my students in understanding text, enhancing reading and writing skills, and organizing their materials. I provided quite a lot of assistance when we first started; however, as they have become more skilled, they've become able to complete this process independently and generate their own type of map for the designated text. This tactic of mapping works for all students in my classroom but is especially important for those with lower reading and writing comprehension levels.

Carina T., teacher

Benefits: When students use story maps, they

- comprehend more of the assigned written text because they can break it down into smaller, more understandable units;
- can organize information with great skill and, consequently, improve their spoken and written language; and
- develop a more positive self-image and enhance their self-esteem as they have greater academic success.

RTI Accommodations/Modifications:

> *Tier I:*
>
> - Model making idea maps for all students;
> - develop and post acronyms that would help students remember strategies; and/or
> - use the strategy repeatedly—across content areas, classes, and tasks—to give students additional practice.
>
> *Tier II:*
>
> - Monitor student use of the tactic;
> - organize students into small groups or dyads to create maps together; and/or
> - use other graphic organizers, such as outlines or syllabi, to practice mapping.
>
> *Tier III:*
>
> - Modify maps to make them less or more complex, based on individual student needs;
> - use text that is at or below a student's reading level; and/or
> - use student interests and skills in selecting text for making idea maps.

Literature:

Baker, S. K., Chard, D. J., Ketterlin-Geller, L. R., Apichatabutra, C., & Doabler, C. (2009). Teaching writing to at-risk students: The quality of evidence for self-regulated strategy development. *Exceptional Children, 75,* 303–318.

Boulineau, T., Fore III, C., Hagan-Burke, S., & Burke, M. D. (2004). Use of story-mapping to increase the story-grammar text comprehension of elementary students with learning disabilities. *Learning Disability Quarterly, 27,* 105–120.

Vallecorsa, A. L., & deBettencourt, L. U. (1997). Using a mapping procedure to teach reading and writing skills to middle grade students with learning disabilities. *Education and Treatment of Children, 20,* 173–188.

Idea Map

Name _____   **Date**_____

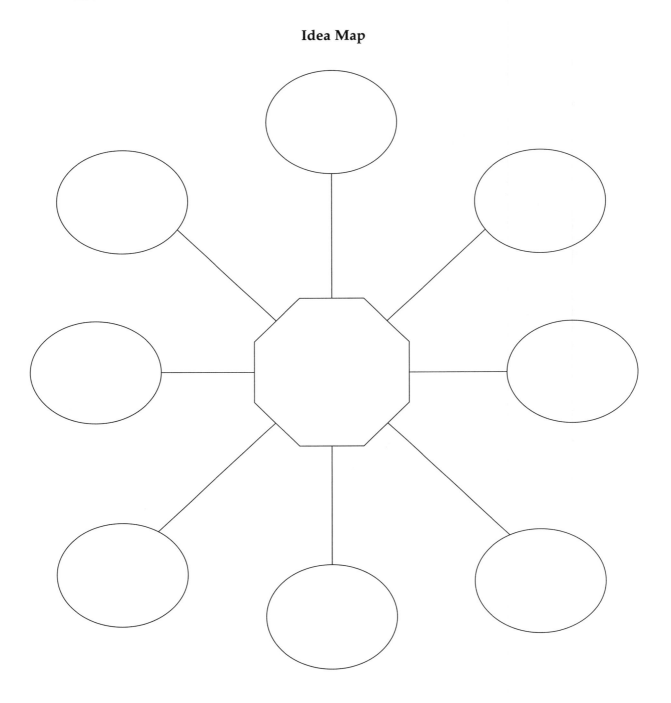

Idea Map

SOURCE: Algozzine, B., Campbell, P., & Wang, A. (2009b). *63 tactics for teaching students with diverse needs: K–6.* Thousand Oaks, CA: Corwin.

Chapter 7: Present Information

Strategy:	Teach Divergent Thinking

Learning Difference:	Cognition Low; Cognition Mixed; Receptive Language/Decoding (listening, reading); Expressive Language/Encoding (speaking, writing, spelling); Fine Motor (handwriting, articulation, etc.); Processing Visual Information

Tactic Title:	Share What You See

Problem: Some students with comprehension or expressive language issues find it difficult to participate in free writing or writing from a written prompt.

Tactic: First, gather a collection of books or texts that incorporate pictures and/or graphic representations of information. "Hide" the text. Together with students, review the pictures/graphics and discuss possible interpretations of their meanings. Encourage students to make notes. Then, use the writing process (brainstorm, outline, draft, review, edit, revise, finalize, publish) to create text that supports/explains the pictures/graphics. Share student products. Reveal the text and compare it with the student versions. Discuss and validate the differences in their thinking.

Example: I love using this tactic as an alternative way to allow students to explore and use their individual creativity in ways that we all benefit from. I've used it in reading, science, social studies, and other content areas. However, I've found it especially instructive when we have an opportunity to explore a needed "social dilemma/situation." The interpretations of my students are very revealing and helpful in resolving issues that might have been potentially more explosive. Nice way to integrate thinking skills, writing, and social skills into a single learning experience. Although, I have to admit that we all get so engrossed in the process and the products, a single issue might result in several days of learning activities—not a bad thing when so much learning was being accomplished across multiple learning objectives.

Julienne W., teacher

Benefits: Using pictorial/graphic representations to encourage divergent thinking

- gives students the freedom to think creatively;
- validates the reasons for their selections; and
- addresses diverse learning interests, needs, and abilities simultaneously.

RTI Accommodations/Modifications:

Tier I:

- Model an example of the thinking process for all students;
- model note taking; and/or
- post writing process steps for everyone to see at all times.

Tier II:

- Give small groups or pairs of students fewer pictures;
- provide alternative response methods; and/or
- monitor discussions and provide supportive/informative feedback.

Tier III:

- Provide two or three pictures as the basis for learning the divergent thinking process;
- model the divergent thinking process aloud with individual students; and/or
- use individual student interests as the focus for activities.

Literature:

Huang, E. (2009). Teaching button-pushing versus teaching thinking: The state of new media education in U.S. universities. *Convergence, 15,* 233–247.

Mettas, A., & Constantinou, C. (2008). The technology fair: A project-based learning approach for enhancing problem solving skills and interest in design and technology education. *Journal of Technology and Design Education, 18*(1), 79–100.

Osburn, H. (2006). Creativity and planning: Training interventions to develop creative problem-solving skills. *Creativity Research Journal, 18,* 173–190.

Chapter 7: **Present Information**

Strategy:	**Teach Learning Strategies**
Learning Difference:	Study Skills; Memory Long-term; Receptive Language/Decoding (listening, reading); Cognition Mixed; Cognition Low; Cognition High

Tactic Title:	**Increasing Recall With Mnemonics**
Problem:	Students, especially those with learning disabilities, frequently have difficulty sorting through and remembering the material they are required to learn.
Tactic:	First, take a piece of information or a concept that may be difficult to remember and simplify it as much as possible so that the amount and complexity of reading are reduced but the idea remains intact. Next, take key words from the fact or idea and relate them to words that are more familiar to the student. For example, the scientific classification of organisms—Kingdom, Phylum, Class, Order, Family, Genus, Species—can be made easier to remember by taking the first letter of each word and making a phrase or sentence out of different words that start with the same letters (e.g., **K**ings **P**lay **C**hess **O**n **F**ine **G**reen **S**ilk). This is a mnemonic letter strategy. Then, to increase the ease of recall even further, associate the new phrase or sentence with a picture or cartoon that illustrates the idea. Finally, as students become more familiar with this strategy, let them develop their own mnemonic devices, as those they develop on their own have more meaning and are even more effective than those provided by others.
Example:	One of the more familiar applications of this tactic has been used to teach the names of the planets: **M**y **V**ery **E**xcellent **M**other **J**ust **S**ent **U**s **N**ew **P**ancakes (Mars, Venus, Earth, Mercury, Jupiter, Saturn, Uranus, Neptune, Pluto). (Of course, Pluto is no longer a planet, so perhaps Mother now has to send us nachos.) It's also been modified to a single word to help students remember the names of the Great Lakes: HOMES (Huron, Ontario, Michigan, Erie, Superior). I've used this tactic to teach the spelling of the /ir/ sound to students. The sound /ir/ can be spelled as *er*, *ir*, or *ur*. However, many fewer words are spelled with *ur*. So I taught my students a "silly sentence" that incorporates some of those words: "Do not dist**ur**b the n**ur**se with the p**ur**ple f**ur**ry t**ur**tle on Thursday." I let students use other *ur* words to make up their own sentences. *Emilio R., teacher*
Benefits:	Mnemonics enable students to • increase the length of time they are able to remember facts; • increase the amount of information they are able to recall on demand; and • foster their creative thinking.

RTI Accommodations/Modifications:

      Tier I:

- Create mnemonics for terms that everyone needs to remember;
- post mnemonics and spot check regularly; and/or
- integrate the use of terms across curricula.

      Tiers II & III:

- Develop instructional games incorporating mnemonics for individuals and small groups of students;
- teach students how to create their own mnemonics; and/or
- practice and monitor daily.

Literature:

Deshler, D. D., Ellis, E. S., & Lenz, B. K. (1996). *Teaching adolescents with learning disabilities* (2nd ed.). Denver: Love.

Deshler, D. D., Schumaker, J. B., & Woodruff, S. K. (2004). Improving literacy skills of at-risk adolescents: A schoolwide response. In D. S. Strickland & D. E. Alvermann (Eds.), *Bridging the literacy achievement gap grades 4–12* (pp. 86–106). New York: Teachers College Press.

Mastropieri, M. A., & Scruggs, T. E. (1998). Enhancing school success with mnemonic strategies. *Intervention in School and Clinic, 33,* 201–208.

Chapter 7: **Present Information**

Strategy:	**Develop Automaticity**

Learning Difference: Study Skills; Memory Long-term; Receptive Language/Decoding (listening, reading); Cognition Mixed; Cognition Low; Cognition High

Tactic Title:	**Using Learning Centers to Refine Skills**

Problem: If students are to use learned skills, they must become proficient by developing automaticity. It is not sufficient to be "fairly accurate" and/ or "fairly rapid in responding." They must have *both* high accuracy *and* high speed. Otherwise, they will not be able to use the skill effectively.

Tactic: Organize learning centers that give students additional opportunities throughout the school day to increase rates and accuracy. Students must be ready to move from the Acquisition learning phase to the Proficiency phase of learning (See Table 2: Instructional Planning and Learning Phases in the Preface); otherwise, they could be practicing errors. However, using peers as tutors/learning partners and self- or student-correcting materials can reduce the likelihood of "error practice." Use games, playing cards, and/or computers to provide fast-paced drill and practice sessions that focus on skills that need to be refined in terms of accuracy and speed. Provide activities that move from guided to independent practice and rely less often on teacher, paraprofessional, or peer interventions. Once students are proficient using a skill, consider ways to move them to the Maintenance and Generalization phases of learning.

Example: I've taught at several different grade levels and in two content areas (math and science). I've always used centers because they can offer so many different instructional tools simultaneously: computers, independent practice, peer tutors, art/music/drama, silent reading . . . the list goes on. In addition, I can provide assignments that are designed specifically for individual students, based on their needs, and incorporate accommodations as well. Centers free me to become more engaged in how my students are learning, as well as to arrange small-group and/ or individual lessons. One important caveat: You must introduce each center carefully and teach students how to use it. Posting instructions/ reminders at each center has really helped.

Joshua F., teacher

Benefits: Learning centers

- can be individualized according to learning objectives and individual student abilities/needs;
- provide excellent opportunities for guided practice (with a skilled partner) or independent practice; and
- reinforce concepts and skills in a wide variety of presentation and response modes.

RTI Accommodations/Modifications:

> *Tier I:*
>
> • Teach learning center activities to students prior to use;
> • integrate one-minute timings and have students chart data; and/or
> • use software that records and prints records of student performance.
>
> *Tier II:*
>
> • Create learning center activities that involve partners or groups of three or four students;
> • post instructions for activities in learning centers; and/or
> • ensure that activities can be modified to meet the needs of different partners/small groups.
>
> *Tier III:*
>
> • Modify learning center activities to meet the needs of individual learners;
> • require daily practice sessions; and/or
> • review learning center performance data with students regularly.

Literature:

Ellis, E. S., & Worthington, L. A. (1994). *Research synthesis on effective teaching principles and the design of quality tools for educators* (Technical Report No. 5). Eugene: University of Oregon, National Center to Improve the Tools of Educators.

King-Sears, M. E. (2007). Designing and delivering learning center instruction. *Intervention in School and Clinic, 42,* 137–147.

Tomlinson, C. A. (2004). *The differentiated classroom: Responding to the needs of all learners.* Upper Saddle River, NJ: Prentice-Hall.

Chapter 7: **Present Information**

Strategy:	**Vary Opportunities for Practice/Vary Methods of Practice**

Learning Difference: Receptive Language/Decoding (listening, reading)

Tactic Title:	**Reading Aloud to Enhance Comprehension of English**

Problem: English-language learners (ELLs) are often frustrated when they are expected to comprehend written material immediately.

Tactic: If students cannot read English well, they must decode and translate words while comprehending the meaning of the vocabulary, sentences, and paragraphs. Therefore, finding alternatives to reading alone or aloud in front of others is essential. Give ELLs colored highlighters or small colored sticky notes. Select competent readers. Let your second-language learners read along as others read aloud. Stop now and then to discuss vocabulary that is critical to comprehension, identify the main idea and supporting details, hypothesize together about the author's intent and other reading concepts. ELLs can use the sticky notes or highlighters to note individual words, main ideas, and so forth so that when they read independently, they will have cues. At the end of the lesson, have ELLs record words in their personal English dictionaries.

Benefits: Giving ELLs the opportunity to listen to others read and discuss written material

- provides a safe preview activity;
- provides models of accurate and fluent reading; and
- enhances comprehension.

RTI Accommodations/Modifications:

Tier I:

- Use choral reading as well as individual readers;
- preteach new vocabulary; and/or
- use texts that value diversity in terms of cultures, languages, ethnicities, and disabilities.

Tier II:

- Use taped books in learning centers;
- use partner-reading; and/or
- provide graphic organizers.

Tier III:

- Modify reading selections via color-coding;
- provide gloss notes to point out main ideas and other important information;
- provide text in ELLs' native language(s) first; and/or
- monitor comprehension frequently.

Literature: Díaz-Rico, L. T., & Weed, K. Z. (in press). *The crosscultural, language, and academic handbook: A complete K–12 reference guide* (4th ed.). Boston: Allyn & Bacon/Pearson.

Mercer, C. D., & Mercer, A. R. (2005). *Teaching students with learning problems* (7th ed.). Columbus, OH: Merrill/Prentice Hall.

Rothstein-Fisch, C., Greenfield, P. M., & Trumbull, E. (1999). Bridging cultures with classroom strategies. *Educational Leadership, 56,* 64–67.

Chapter 7: **Present Information**

Strategy:	**Monitor Amount of Work Assigned**

Learning Difference: Attention; Self-confidence

Tactic Title:	**Modify Assignments**

Problem: Some students can accomplish more with less. In other words, work that is too difficult or tasks that are designed to be accomplished over time can be especially challenging for some students. To enable these students to be more successful, assignments need to be modified.

Tactic: For tasks that are too difficult, review prior work to determine appropriate instructional levels. Discuss options with the student to reach consensus. Options may include additional review of material, reducing the number of items in or the length of an assignment, or providing additional time. For assignments that may seem too lengthy in terms of days, break the assignment into smaller segments to be completed in shorter increments of time. Finally, try to make assignments more interesting or personal.

Example: I have several students who also see the special education teacher, Shirley, for math. Due to visual memory deficits, they've had a difficult time mastering their multiplication tables, and these facts are the basis for moving on to more difficult mathematics. So I break their worksheets into two parts: one part to be completed with the other students in the class and the second part to be completed later with Shirley. Sometimes, we reverse the order, especially when she can preteach a skill to be taught in my class the following day.

Alexandria O'N., teacher

Benefits: When assignments are modified, students

- are more motivated;
- are more successful; and
- feel more confident.

RTI Accommodations/Modifications:

Tier I:

- Provide flexible due dates;
- provide opportunities for self-correction; and/or
- gradually increase task length and complexity.

Tier II:

- Let students complete assignments in small groups or dyads;
- give students specific tasks/roles/responsibilities when completing a group activity; and/or
- provide an assignment "menu" outlining components of the task and reasonable due dates.

Tier III:

- Provide supplemental/supportive learning center activities;
- provide an alternative assignment; and/or
- develop a personal calendar or schedule with student.

Literature:

Fulk, D. J., & Montgomery-Grymes, D. J. (1994). Strategies to improve student motivation. *Intervention in School and Clinic, 30,* 28–33.

Mellard, D. F., & Johnson, E. (2008). *RTI: A practitioner's guide to implementing response to intervention.* Thousand Oaks, CA: Corwin.

Morgan, M., & Moni, K. B. (2007). Motivate students with disabilities using sight-vocabulary activities. *Intervention in School and Clinic, 4,* 229–233.

Tomlinson, C. A. (2004). *The differentiated classroom: Responding to the needs of all learners.* Upper Saddle River, NJ: Prentice-Hall.

8

Monitor Presentations

Principle	Strategy
Monitor Presentations	*Providing Feedback*
	Give Immediate, Frequent, Explicit Feedback/Provide Specific Praise and Encouragement
	Model Correct Performance
	Provide Prompts and Cues
	Check Student Understanding
	Keeping Students Actively Involved
	Monitor Performance Regularly/Monitor Performance During Practice
	Use Peers to Improve Instruction
	Provide Opportunities for Success/Limit Opportunities for Failure
	Monitor Engagement Rates

Chapter 8: Monitor Presentations

Strategy:	Give Immediate, Frequent, Explicit Feedback/Provide Specific Praise and Encouragement

Learning Difference: Attention; Expressive Language/Encoding (speaking, writing, spelling)

Tactic Title:	Listen-Sketch-Discuss (LSD)

Problem: Frequently, students have difficulty taking notes from text because of the time needed to process the information and formulate how to put those ideas on paper.

Tactic: Have the students take out a sheet of paper and divide the paper into a number blocks, depending upon the number of paragraphs they will be reading. Then, read each paragraph aloud while the students sketch pictures of what they are hearing. After each paragraph, students pair up with "buddies" and discuss what they have drawn. Ask students either to write a sentence about their drawing or label the sketch with key vocabulary words.

Example: This is a variation of the Lecture-Pause technique that I've used for years, especially with my older students, as well as those who have difficulty taking notes. I only talk/lecture for a maximum of 10 minutes at a time. Then, I pause and give my students three minutes to review their notes, compare theirs with those of a peer, and make any necessary corrections. We address student questions for another two or three minutes. Of course, I adjust the discussion and question time frames as needed. I know that my students understand the material more quickly and accurately; we can see it in the quality of the work they produce.

Eleni R., teacher

Benefits: Giving students time to process verbal information

- increases the quality of their work;
- fosters greater time-on-task; and
- teaches them the importance of reflection, discussion, and clarification.

RTI Accommodations/Modifications:

   Tier I:

- Model/role-play/practice tactic;
- post procedures; and/or
- provide immediate feedback and praise.

   Tier II:

- Modify this tactic to use in small groups or dyads;
- provide less "talk" and more time for review/questions; and/or
- provide graphic organizers, such as outlines or syllabi, to guide note taking/discussion.

Tier III:

- Modify tactic for use with individual students;
- use alternative content; and/or
- begin with shorter segments that are gradually lengthened.

Literature:

Dyson, B. J. (2008). Assessing small-scale interventions in large-scale teaching: A general methodology and preliminary data. *Active Learning in Higher Education, 9,* 265–282.

Hattie, J., & Timperley, H. (2007). The power of feedback. *Review of Educational Research, 77,* 81–112.

Parris, S. R., & Block, C. C. (2007). The expertise of adolescent literacy teachers. *Journal of Adolescent & Adult Literacy, 50,* 582–596.

Rosenshine, B., & Stevens, R. (1986). Teaching functions. In M. C. Wittrock (Ed.), *Handbook of research on teaching* (3rd ed.; pp. 376–391). New York: Macmillan.

Rowe, M. B. (1986). Wait time: Slowing down may be a way of speeding up! *Journal of Teacher Education, 37,* 43–50.

Sugai, G. (2005, November). *Establishing a continuum of support inside the classroom.* Paper presented at the annual Making Connections Conference, Vancouver, BC, Canada.

Werts, M. G., Caldwell, N. K., & Wolery, M. (2003). Instructive feedback: Effects of a presentation variable. *Journal of Special Education, 37,* 124–133.

Chapter 8: Monitor Presentations

Strategy:	**Model Correct Performance**

Learning Difference: Attention; Expressive Language/Encoding (speaking, writing, spelling); Processing Verbal Information

Tactic Title:	**Your Pictures Tell the Story**

Problem: Finding creative ways to introduce the components of narrative text can be challenging.

Tactic: Pick a writing topic that is interesting and relevant to your students. Then, review and briefly discuss the types of narrative text: fiction (realistic fiction, science fiction, mysteries, folktales, fairy tales, and myths) or nonfiction (reports, factual stories, and biographies). Next, discuss the common components of narrative text:

1. Setting: Time, place

2. Characters: Major, minor

3. Plot: Sequence of events (problem, events, solution)

4. Theme: Central idea of the story

5. Vocabulary: Words used to enrich understanding of the story

Then, briefly discuss other considerations such as the author's purpose(s) for writing the story and the literary devices (author's choices regarding vocabulary chosen and the use of imagery, figurative language, foreshadowing, and flashback).

Before reading the story to your students, ask them to divide a blank sheet of unlined paper into the number of sections that corresponds to the number of parts of the following that you will be using:

• Each of the five components
• Each of the characters
• The sequence of major events
• Vocabulary
• Examples of imagery, figurative language, foreshadowing, and flashback
• Another topic of your choice

Model drawing a picture to represent each of the sections. Talk about your thinking processes as you model for your students. Then, read the narrative text to your students and have them create a picture to represent each of the sections/topics. As you read, walk around the classroom to monitor student progress. Provide support and/or corrective feedback as needed. At the conclusion of the activity, provide closure via a discussion of student thinking processes and their final products.

Example: I try to use visuals to reinforce student learning as much as possible. While the tactic as written seems designed for students in the elementary grades, I've used a similar idea with my secondary students—just enhanced it a bit. I've generated handouts on the computer and used podcasts to enable my students to listen to narrative text and complete the activity for homework. Of course, I use literature and nonfiction pieces that are appropriate for secondary students. Thus, they are able to upload their own artwork or generate/find artistic representations that fulfill the requirements of the assignment. Now, I'm expanding to using this idea with expository text and encouraging my students to post their final products for their peers.

Zoe P., teacher

Benefits: When students use pictures to illustrate the components of a story, they

- use their thinking skills in reverse order; typically, they preview illustrations to inform their reading of written text;
- are able to use creative thinking and talents; and
- have the freedom to interpret text in individual ways.

RTI Accommodations/Modifications:

   Tier I:

   - Modify the assignment to focus on fewer components of narrative text;
   - post key components for easy access/review; and/or
   - use the strategy across content areas and types of text to give students additional practice.

   Tier II:

   - Monitor student use of the tactic and provide ongoing feedback;
   - organize students into small groups or dyads to create maps together; and/or
   - reduce the required number of components.

   Tier III:

   - Modify maps to make them less or more complex, based on individual student needs;
   - use text that is at or below a student's reading level; and/or
   - use other graphic organizers, such as outlines or syllabi, to practice mapping.

Literature: Adamson, H. (1993). *Academic competence.* New York: Longman.

   Campbell, P., & Siperstein, G. P. (1994). *Developing social competence: A resource for elementary teachers.* Boston: Allyn & Bacon.

   Carnine, D. W., Silbert, J., Kame'enui, E. F., & Tarver, S. G. (2004). *Direct instruction reading* (4th ed.). Upper Saddle River, NJ: Pearson/Merrill Prentice Hall.

   Díaz-Rico, L. T., & Weed, K. Z. (in press). *The crosscultural, language, and academic handbook: A complete K–12 reference guide* (4th ed.). Boston: Allyn & Bacon/Pearson.

   Miller, S. P. (2009). *Validated practices for teaching students with diverse needs and abilities* (2nd ed.). Upper Saddle River, NJ: Pearson.

Chapter 8: **Monitor Presentations**

Strategy:	**Provide Prompts and Cues**

Learning Difference: Attention; Study Skills

Tactic Title:	**Homework Modification**

Problem: Frequently, students have difficulty planning their time or concentrating on homework assignments.

Tactic: Divide the assignment into sections. When you are ready to present the assignment to your students, distribute highlighters, markers, colored pencils, or crayons together with the assignment. Then, as you model on an overhead or computer projector or smart-, white-, or chalkboard, ask students to draw vertical lines in the left-hand margin that correspond to the sections that you have decided upon. For example, with a mathematics worksheet, section 1 might be computation (coded in yellow), section 2 might be word problems (coded in blue), and so forth. Distribute a schedule. (Use the Homework Planner worksheet on page 106.) With the students, fill in the required information (name, assignment, date assigned, date due, estimated total time needed, section titles). Then, tell students to estimate and fill in the time needed for each section and the time they plan to start the assignment. Finally, tell students to record their individual section time completed information in the appropriate boxes, together with a brief reflection/plan statement, and submit the form with their homework.

Example: So many of my students struggle with homework because of their lack of time management skills or issues with focus and attention. So I've found this Homework Planner very helpful in letting all of us plan together to make homework useful and doable. However, being on the same page as the other colleagues who work with my students and my students' parents, I've added signature lines to the bottom of the form for them to sign off that they have reviewed the completed form and agree. OK . . . I'll admit that I had another motive. My students know that others also care that they do well. It really doesn't take a lot of my time . . . and once I've taken a look at their completed forms, I know so much more about them and what they need. They then file these forms in a special folder to document their progress throughout the year.

Nikhil R., teacher

Benefits: When prompts and cues are provided for students, they are able to

- complete more assignments correctly and on time;
- learn how to organize their time and focus on responsibilities; and/or
- actually find more time for other activities—those that previously caused the interruptions that delayed and/or distracted them from completing homework.

RTI Accommodations/Modifications:

> *Tier I:*
>
> - Provide assignments that are already color-coded;
> - upload assignments onto the Internet or a classroom computer for easy accessibility;
> - use the strategy repeatedly—across content areas, classes, and tasks—to give students additional practice; and/or
> - provide bonus points for completion, thoughtful reflections, etc.
>
> *Tier II:*
>
> - Organize students into small groups or dyads to complete Homework Planner worksheets together;
> - require student sign-off signatures; and/or
> - modify the amount of material.
>
> *Tier III:*
>
> - Collaborate with parents/paraprofessionals who might be involved;
> - use text that is at or below a student's reading level; and/or
> - modify by using graphic labels.

Literature:

DuPaul, G. J., Gardill, M. C., & Kyle, K. E. (1996). Classroom strategies for managing students with ADHD. *Intervention in School and Clinic, 32,* 89–94.

Epstein, M., Polloway, E., Buck, G., Bursuck, W., Wissinger, L., Whitehouse, F., et al. (1997). Homework-related communication problems: Perspectives of general education teachers. *Learning Disabilities Research and Practice, 12,* 221–227.

Joseph, L. M., & Konrad, M. (2009). Have students self-manage their academic performance. *Intervention in School and Clinic, 44,* 246–249.

Homework Planner

Name: _____   **Assignment:**_____

Date Assigned:_____   **Date Due:**_____   **Estimated Total Time Needed:**_____

Time Needed	Time Started	Section	Time Completed	Time Taken (+/-)	Reflection/Plan
Example: 20 mins.	7:00 PM	1. Computation (colored in yellow)	7:30	+ 10 mins.	Think they're correct, but took too long—got interrupted. Need to turn off phone.

Chapter 8: Monitor Presentations

Strategy:	**Check Student Understanding**
Learning Difference:	Attention; Memory Short-term; Memory Long-term; Receptive Language/Decoding (listening, reading); Processing Verbal Information

Tactic Title:	**Outlining and Visualizing Lessons**
Problem:	Many students have difficulty following verbal directions and transitioning, even after detailed task instructions have been provided. Consequently, precious time can be wasted re-explaining tasks.
Tactic:	To avoid transition problems and help all students follow directions, do the following:

1. Outline the steps of the lesson on the board for all the students to visualize *before* you give the lesson. Here is an example:

   a. Brainstorm adjectives as a class on the floor.

   b. Return to desks and write a short paragraph.

   c. Edit the paragraph.

   d. Draw a picture.

   e. When finished, leave the paragraph on your desk and finish morning work.

2. Begin the lesson by explaining to the students all the steps of the lesson. Provide an overview of what they will be doing. Tell the students you wrote the steps on the board.

3. Deliver the lesson.

4. Review the steps of the lesson. If the lesson is a multitask project, you may occasionally say to the class: "Now we are doing . . ." and point to the step on the board so students are aware of their progress as the lesson proceeds. If the lesson is like the example above, where the students are asked to work independently, it is a good idea to review the steps before sending students to work independently.

Example:	I've found that a visual aid such as this is especially helpful for students who have difficulty retaining or processing verbal information. By having an outline of a lesson plan to see and review, they transition between tasks without wasting time to ask questions such as, "What do I do next?" "What am I supposed to do again?" And I can be working with individual or small groups of students without having to stop to re-explain the tasks.

Sean T., teacher

Benefits: Providing a visual outline of tasks

- saves instructional time;
- increases student time-on-task; and
- provides a nonverbal cue that is not disruptive to the learning of others.

RTI Accommodations/Modifications:

Tier I:

- Ask students to repeat instructions; and/or
- provide student planners for long-term projects/tasks.

Tier II:

- Place students in groups with heterogeneous learning skills or needs;
- give groups specific locations for working; and/or
- ensure that groups have all needed materials prior to beginning the activity.

Tier III:

- Review instructions with the student;
- post instructions on student desk or in work folder; and/or
- monitor student progress throughout the activity.

Literature: Griffiths, A.-M., VanDerHeyden, A. M., Parson, L. B., & Burns, M. K. (2008). Examination of the utility of various measures of mathematics proficiency. *Learning Disabilities, 34,* 34–58.

Rock, M. L., & Thead, B. K. (2009). Promote student success during independent seatwork. *Intervention in School and Clinic, 44,* 179–184.

Chapter 8: Monitor Presentations

Strategy:	**Monitor Performance Regularly/Monitor Performance During Practice**

Learning Difference: Attention; Self-control; Self-confidence; Social Behaviors

Tactic Title:	**Private Teacher-Student Conferences**

Problem: Some students need extra reassurance and attention to be successful academically and/or behaviorally.

Tactic: Taking the time to meet one-on-one with students can provide additional support for them. Build time into your schedule to meet with individual students on a regular basis. Oftentimes, five minutes every other week is sufficient. Encourage students to express any concerns or questions that they have. Teach students to tell you about their accomplishments. Discuss students strengths and needs. Provide specific examples of progress that you have observed before discussing issues/concerns. Make a plan and schedule the next conference. End the conference on a positive note.

Example: I use some student conferences to plan how we will conduct a future parent/teacher conference. At other times, we focus on academic work or behavior. Oftentimes, we talk about social relationships with other students. The focus really depends on the individual student, and that is what makes the conferences so important. At first, I was reluctant to give up "instructional time," but then I realized that I was still teaching when conferencing. So it really is worth the time.

Eric G., teacher

Benefits: Monitoring performance through individual student conferences enables

- issues of immediate concern to be addressed in a timely manner;
- teachers to provide the positive support that many students need; and
- students to see and feel clearly that their teachers care about them and truly want them to succeed.

RTI Accommodations/Modifications:

Tier I:

- Use portfolios as the basis for conversation;
- schedule individual conferences as frequently as needed; and/or
- teach students to take responsibility for leading the discussion.

Tier II:

- Meet with teams or pairs of students to review the process of their working together;
- use the time to resolve problems with academic or behavior issues; and/or
- record plans and promises made during the meeting and schedule the next conference.

Tier III:

- Keep a running record of the topics discussed with individual students;
- when dealing with behavior, record future plans and strategies, sign and date and have the student sign and date, and schedule a future date for review of progress; and/or
- teach students to reflect on the performance (academic or behavioral) since the previous conference.

Literature:

DuPaul, G. J., & Kyle, K. E. (1996). Classroom strategies for managing students with ADHD. *Intervention in School and Clinic, 32,* 318–319.

Marzano, R. J. (2003). *Classroom management that works: Research-based strategies for every teacher.* Alexandria, VA: Association for Supervision and Curriculum Development.

Mechling, L. C. (2007). Assistive technology as a self-management tool for prompting students with intellectual disabilities to initiate and complete daily tasks: A literature review. *Education and Training in Developmental Disabilities, 42,* 252–269.

Chapter 8: **Monitor Presentations**

Strategy:	**Use Peers to Improve Instruction**
Learning Difference:	Study Skills; Self-confidence; Expressive Language/Encoding (speaking, writing, spelling); Receptive Language/Decoding (listening, reading)

Tactic Title:	**Implementing a Classwide Peer Buddy System**
Problem:	Teachers often find that students become more self-concious and insecure about their academic abilities when they are singled out for extra help.
Tactic:	Divide your class into dyads based on the learning goals so that the pairs can be determined by academic needs, social needs, behavioral tendencies, and so forth. Train all students in effective tutoring strategies. During tutoring sessions, each student tutors his or her partner with a certain set of problems or examples. As students are engaged in a tutoring session, circulate, observing both learning and the tutoring process. You may decide to award points for following tutoring procedures correctly. These procedures might include checking for understanding, cooperating, listening, following directions, and checking work. You might also decide to implement "Each One, Teach One," where you teach one student how to tutor and when you observe that student tutoring correctly, have that student teach a classmate how to tutor. Repeat the process.
Example:	It took a little time to teach the tutoring process to them; however, it's been worth it. The tutors use the laminated cue cards that I created to check off each step as they tutor:

1. Organize materials.

2. Introduce the activity.

3. Give directions.

4. Check for understanding.

5. Monitor tutee's work.

6. Provide supportive/corrective feedback.

7. Praise effort.

8. Summarize activity.

9. Reflect on tutoring process together.

I believe that everyone should have the experience of being tutored, as well as being the tutor. Being a tutor can really boost self-esteem. So we also reverse roles. Sometimes having to teach something to another person forces you to learn it well yourself.

Talia M., teacher

Benefits: Implementing a classwide peer buddy system

- provides extra support for students;
- fosters collaboration among classmates; and
- benefits both the tutee and the tutor.

RTI Accommodations/Modifications:

Tier I:

- Integrate a classwide peer buddy system across different content areas;
- teach tutors how to tutor and monitor their tutoring; and/or
- use grouping charts (see the tactic "Establish Grouping Structures" in Chapter 2) to determine pairs.

Tier II:

- Modify the pairs according to the content area and student needs/skills;
- provide graphic organizers that list tutoring procedures to be followed; and/or
- have students reflect on the tutoring process and share ways in which it might be improved.

Tier III:

- Teach *all* students how to tutor and be tutored;
- modify the tutoring process according to student needs; and/or
- modify content, time frame, number of sessions, and materials.

Literature: Allsopp, D. H. (1997). Using classwide peer tutoring to teach beginning algebra problem-solving skills in heterogeneous classrooms. *Remedial and Special Education, 18,* 367–379.

Calhoun, M. B., Otaiba, S. A., Cihak, D., King, A., & Avalos, A. (2007). Effects of a peer-mediated program on reading skill acquisition for two-way bilingual first-grade classrooms. *Learning Disability Quarterly, 30,* 169-180.

Hughes, T. A., & Fredrick, L. D. (2006). Teaching vocabulary with students with learning disabilities using classwide peer tutoring and constant time delay. *Journal of Behavioral Education, 15,* 1–23.

Mastropieri, M. A., Scruggs, T. E., Norland, J. J., Berkeley, S., McDuffie, K., Tornquist, E. H., et al. (2006). Differentiated curriculum enhancement in inclusive middle school science: Effects on classroom and high-stakes tests. *The Journal of Special Education, 40,* 130–137.

Saenz, L. M., Fuchs, L. S., & Fuchs, D. (2005). Peer-assisted learning strategies for English language learners with learning disabilities. *Exceptional Children, 71,* 231–247.

Veerkamp, M. B., Kamps, D. M., & Cooper, L. (2007). The effects of classwide peer tutoring on the reading achievement of urban middle school students. *Education and Treatment of Children, 30*(2), 21–51.

Chapter 8: Monitor Presentations

Strategies:	**Provide Opportunities for Success/Limit Opportunities for Failure**

Learning Difference: Hearing

Tactic Title:	**Including Students With Hearing Impairments in the Music Classroom.**

Problem: Sometimes it is difficult to include students with hearing impairments in listening exercises in the music classroom.

Tactic: Even though students with hearing impairments may be unable to hear the sounds produced in a recording, they do have the ability to feel vibration. Providing students with hearing impairments a hand-held cassette recorder with ear phones will allow them to feel the vibrations in music through the headphones and still be a part of the class. If this equipment is not available, seat the student as close as possible to audio speakers or the musical instrument being played so the student can put his or her hands on it.

Example: I've also let students with hearing impairments feel the throat of someone who is singing. Sometimes, when I have a paraprofessional in the room, the student touches the throat of the paraprofessional during the song and tries to imitate the sounds or vibration with his or her own throat.

John T., teacher

Benefits: Finding ways to include students with hearing impairments

- enables them to be an integral member of the group;
- models acceptance and inclusive practice for others; and
- enhances opportunities for student learning.

RTI Accommodations/Modifications:

Tier I:

- Use a variety of instruments with varying types of sounds and vibrations;
- modify the organization of your classroom to provide access for the student; and/or
- use sign language in teaching.

Tiers II & III:

- Pair a student with a hearing impairment with a peer buddy to feel vibrations;
- monitor understanding of activities; and/or
- provide visual cues, instructions, and feedback.

Literature: Fairbanks, S., Simonsen, B., & Sugai, G. (2008). Classwide secondary and
                   tertiary tier practices and systems. *TEACHING Exceptional Children,*
                   40(6), 44–52.

                   Garza, R. (2009). Latino and White high school students' perceptions of
                   caring behavior: Are we culturally responsive to our students? *Urban*
                   Education, 44, 237–321.

                   Lee, S.-H., Soukup, J. H., Little, T. D., & Wehmeyer, M. L. (2009). Student
                   and teacher variables contributing to access to the general education
                   curriculum for students with intellectual and developmental disabili-
                   ties. *The Journal of Special Education, 43*(1), 29–44.

                   Osterman, K. F. (2000). Students' need for belonging in the school com-
                   munity. *Review of Educational Research, 70,* 323–367.

Chapter 8: **Monitor Presentations**

Strategy:	**Monitor Engagement Rates**

Learning Difference:	Mobility; Speaking/Talking; Cognition Mixed; Attention; Receptive Language/Decoding (listening, reading); Expressive Language/Encoding (speaking, writing, spelling); Gross Motor (running, walking, etc.); Processing Verbal Information; Study Skills; Social Knowledge; Self-control; Social Behaviors; Self-care; Self-confidence

Tactic Title:	**Three for One**

Problem:	Some students need a little extra planning for, because they either finish assignments quickly or have difficulty remaining on-task.
Tactic:	Plan extra activities for these students. For the student who works more quickly than others, plan related enrichment activities. For the student who has difficulty staying on-task, plan variations on the original activity that enable the student to move to another location, use manipulatives, engage in a listening activity, or work with a peer. As you monitor your students' engagement and see that students are either finished or off-task, move them on to another activity.
Example:	I always plan three activities for one of my students with ADHD. In this way, when he begins to lose his attention, I simply switch him to another task. For instance, we began the other day by writing three sentences about the rain forest. After his first sentence, he had completely lost interest. Therefore, while the other students continued with their sentences, he switched to a frog-finding activity that involved counting the frogs once he found them (math skills). When he had tired of that, after only about five minutes, we switched to an activity in which he had to place different animals in the layer of the rain forest in which they live. Then he went back to writing, and so on. Eventually, he did complete all three tasks.

Larissa B., teacher

Benefits:	When teachers monitor student engagement rates, they can

- adjust the assignment;
- differentiate instruction to meet individual student needs; and
- enhance opportunities for student achievement.

RTI Accommodations/Modifications:

    Tier I:

- Plan a variety of activities that take advantage of different learning styles;
- modify response modes; and/or
- use this tactic across content areas.

Tier II:

- Move students into small groups or dyads;
- divide activities into smaller sections with alternative tasks or two-minute "breaks" between sections; and/or
- use graphic organizers, such as outlines, so that students can check off tasks or portions of tasks as completed.

Tier III:

- Provide alternative tasks designed to utilize student interests and abilities;
- provide ongoing supportive encouraging feedback; and/or
- teach the student to self-record on-task behavior to earn a special "academic" reward.

Literature:

Goodlad, J. (2000). Education and democracy: Advancing the agenda. *Phi Delta Kappan, 82*(1), 86–89.

Greenwood, C. R., Horton, B. T., & Utley, C. A. (2002). Academic engagement: Current perspectives in research and practice. *School Psychology Review, 31*, 328–349.

Seo, S., Brownell, M. T., Bishop, A. G., & Dingle, M. (2008). An examination of beginning special education teachers' classroom practice that engage elementary students with learning disabilities in reading instruction. *Exceptional Children, 75*, 97–122.

9

Adjust Presentations

Principle	Strategy
Adjust Presentations	Adapt Lessons to Meet Student Needs
	Provide Varied Instructional Options
	Alter Pace

Chapter 9: **Adjust Presentations**

Strategy:	**Adapt Lessons to Meet Student Needs**

Learning Difference: Attention; Expressive Language/Encoding (speaking, writing, spelling); Fine Motor (handwriting, articulation, etc.)

Tactic Title:	**Hands-on Activities: Alternatives to Essay Writing**

Problem: Teachers often find that students have difficulty with concentration and attention when assigned to write an extensive essay.

Tactic: Rather than having these students take the traditional approach of writing an essay to describe a specific topic, give them the freedom to choose an alternative hands-on project to share with the class. For example, say students are learning about sharks in science. Some students may be musically oriented and write a song about their knowledge of sharks. An artistic student may make a model or act out a skit about sharks. Others might create a PowerPoint presentation that documents scientific shark explorations (with videos).

Example: I teach art, and recently we've been looking for ways to integrate required academic mathematical concepts (shapes, symbols, pentagrams, etc.) into art. So we've been learning about Leonardo da Vinci and the Italian researcher, G. M. Pala, who believes that da Vinci's *Last Supper* painting contains hidden images/symbols and a musical score. Based on that idea, my students have created drawings with "hidden messages." In addition, I'm collaborating with our music teacher, Sean. In his classes, students are composing music based on the notes representing the letters in their names. Students are so motivated and involved, and collaborating with another teacher is the best!

Mike H., teacher of art

Benefits: Giving students opportunities to explore alternative means of expression

- can enrich the learning of all class members;
- lets all students demonstrate their ability to learn and be successful; and
- enhances student participation and interpersonal relationships in the classroom.

RTI Accommodations/Modifications:

> *Tier I:*
>
> - Give students the freedom to create their own drawings;
> - provide samples and model procedures; and/or
> - integrate other content areas into instruction.

Tier II:

- Let students work in pairs to brainstorm ideas and verify information;
- provide a variety of materials/supplies; and/or
- assign different dyad members specific roles.

Tier III:

- Monitor closely and provide ongoing feedback and support;
- adjust the activity to meet the abilities and interests of individual students; and/or
- provide a graphic organizer of the activity.

Literature:

Dolan, R. P., Hall, T. E., Banerjee, M., Chun, E., & Strangman, N. (2005). Applying principles of universal design to test delivery: The effect of computer-based read-aloud on test performance of high school students with learning disabilities. *Journal of Technology, Learning, and Assessment, 3*(7). Available at http://escholarship.bc.edu/jtla/.

Echevarria, J., Short, D., & Powers, K. (2006). School reform and standards-based education: A model for English-language learners. *The Journal of Educational Research, 99*, 195–210.

Gardner, H. (1999). *Intelligence reframed: Multiple intelligences for the 21st century.* New York: Basic Books.

Mechling, L. C. (2007). Assistive technology as a self-management tool for prompting students with intellectual disabilities to initiate and complete daily tasks: A literature review. *Education and Training in Developmental Disabilities, 42*, 252–269.

Nelson, J. S., Jayanthi, M., Epstein, M. H., & Bursuck, W. D. (2000). Student preferences for adaptations in classroom testing. *Remedial and Special Education, 21*, 41–52.

Salend, S. (2008). *Creating inclusive classrooms: Effective and reflective practices* (6th ed.). Upper Saddle River, NJ: Merrill/Prentice Hall.

Chapter 9: Adjust Presentations

Strategy:	**Provide Varied Instructional Options**

Learning Difference: Attention; Social Knowledge; Self-control; Receptive Language/Decoding (listening, reading); Social Behaviors; Self-confidence

Tactic Title:	**Establish a Supportive, Cooperative Environment Through Cooperative Learning**

Problem: Meeting the diverse needs, abilities, and interests of students can be challenging.

Tactic: Start off slowly when implementing cooperative learning in your classroom. Begin each cooperative learning activity with a teacher-led, whole-class discussion about the various roles (questioner, recorder, speaker, etc.) and cooperation (respecting others' ideas, listening, encouraging, sharing, taking turns, etc.). Then, select students to work in pairs; eventually graduate to larger groups. Organize heterogeneous pairs/groups or use sociometric assessments to learn student preferences. (See the Grouping Chart, Parts I and II, in Chapter 2.) Assign roles and have each group work together on a set activity that results in one collaborative response. At the end of each cooperative activity, take time to reflect on what students learned both academically and interpersonally.

Example: I've used cooperative learning in my chemistry class, where students work in groups in the majority of their lab periods. I've found that the structure of cooperative learning tasks has enabled students with very diverse abilities and levels of interest in science to succeed. Sometimes, I "jigsaw" assignments/tasks: I give different portions of an activity to one group, and each group is then responsible for teaching that information to the rest of the class. You can't assume that students know how to work in cooperative groups. Discussing the roles of participants and expected behaviors is essential. I give students a checklist of expectations and responsibilities so that I can evaluate their progress and performance. I use the checklist to evaluate individual and group performance as well.

Keith A., teacher

Benefits: Cooperative learning is an excellent tool for

- managing behavior and fostering positive interpersonal relationships;
- differentiating instruction; and
- designing tasks and roles so that every student can be successful and valued by classmates.

RTI Accommodations/Modifications:

   Tiers I & II:

- Provide graphic organizers that list the tasks in sequence;
- provide clear and specific descriptions of individual roles and responsibilities; and/or
- assign roles based on student ability.

Literature:

Bender, W. N. (2009). *Differentiating math instruction: Strategies that work for K–8 classrooms.* (2nd ed.). Thousand Oaks, CA: Corwin.

Box, J. A., & Little, D. C. (2003). Cooperative small-group instruction combined with advance organizers and their relationship to self-concept and social studies achievement of elementary school students. *Journal of Instructional Psychology, 30,* 285–287.

Jenkins, J. R., Antil, L. R., Wayne, S. K., & Vadasy, P. F. (2003). How cooperative learning works for special education and remedial students. *Exceptional Children, 69,* 279–292.

Marzano, R. J., Pickering, D. J., & Pollack, J. E. (2001). *Classroom instruction that works: Research-based strategies for increasing student achievement.* Alexandria, VA: Association for Supervision and Curriculum Development.

Oortwijn, M. B., Boekaerts, M., & Vedder, P. (2008). The impact of a cooperative learning experience on pupils' popularity, non-cooperativeness, and interethnic bias in multiethnic elementary schools. *Educational Psychology, 28*(2), 1–11.

Wolford, P. L., Heward, W. L., & Alber, S. R. (2001). Teaching middle school students with learning disabilities to recruit peer assistance during cooperative learning group activities. *Learning Disabilities Research & Practice, 16,* 161–173.

Chapter 9: **Adjust Presentations**

Strategy:	**Alter Pace**

Learning Difference:	Speaking/Talking; Processing Visual Information; Expressive Language/ Encoding (speaking, writing, spelling); Social Behaviors

Tactic Title:	**Relating Mathematics to Real-Life Activities**

Problem:	Frequently, students in elementary schools have difficulty understanding mathematical concepts.
Tactic:	Meaningful instructions and real-life examples of concepts are essential components of effective instruction. Finding ways to provide examples within the classroom can often be challenging. By altering the location of activities, you can alter the pace of instruction and learning. First, arrange your students in groups of two. Second, give each pair a Treasure Hunt worksheet (see sample and blank worksheets on pages. 124 and 125). Students take an on-site field trip around the school to collect math-ematical data. Then, have students count a specific number of objects and record and illustrate their data in a math journal. Students use the data to solve mathematical problems, such as those involving addition and subtraction. Afterwards, students use the objects to verify the answers to the equations. Finally, students create a chart in their math journals to demonstrate the numbers of objects found originally and the number of objects after performing the mathematical procedures.
Example:	We created a Friendship Garden in a section of our preK/kindergarten playground because we wanted to integrate the garden into our curricula and, at the same time, beautify the area. So we've planted a Salsa Garden with cilantro, tomatoes, onions, and peppers, together with marigold, petunias, and a giant sunflower. Once the plants started to grow, we started measuring and charting the data. My students used plastic con-necting cubes; the older students used rulers and, in the case of the sun-flower, a measuring tape and a ladder! My students have recorded their data in their math journals with pictures and graphs. We also used the garden as part of our science, literacy, social studies, and "life skills" cur-ricula. Next year, we're planting a Pizza Garden with spinach, tomatoes, parsley, and broccoli.

Nichola P., teacher

Benefits:	Using realia and field trips

- enables students to see how real-life activities illustrate abstract ideas;
- lets teachers modify the pace of instruction; and/or
- demonstrates that learning can take place anywhere.

RTI Accommodations/Modifications:

Tier I:

- Develop rules and procedures that are specific to the activity and review them with students;
- monitor student attention and behavior during the field trip; and/or
- use field trips across content areas.

Tier II:

- Assign specific roles to partners;
- give students a laminated card (and marker) with brief, clear instructions and/or space to record findings;
- monitor student engagement during the field trip by asking questions about what they are finding.

Literature:

Adams, G. L., & Engelmann, S. (1996). *Research on direct instruction: 25 years beyond DISTAR.* Seattle: Educational Achievement Systems.

Castagno, A. E., & Brayboy, B. M. J. (2008). Culturally responsive schooling for indigenous youth: A review of the literature. *Review of Educational Research, 78,* 941–993.

Pianta, R. C., Belsky, J., Vandergrift, N., Houts, R., & Morrison, F. J. (2008). Classroom effects on children's achievement trajectories in elementary school. *American Educational Research Journal, 45,* 365–397.

Walshaw, M., & Anthony, G. (2008). The teacher's role in classroom discourse: A review of recent research into mathematics classrooms. *Review of Educational Research, 78,* 516–551.

Treasure Hunt Worksheet (Sample)

Instructions for Teachers: A sample of items is provided below. Use the blank worksheet to create a Treasure Hunt that meets your needs.

Instructions for Students: Hunt for the objects listed below. Record your data in the right-hand column.

Look for . . .	Count . . .
1. The number of trees on the playground	
2. The number of classrooms on the first floor	
3. The number of male teachers	
4. The number of female teachers	
5. The number of computers in the library	
6. The length of the hallway outside your classroom	
7. The height of the teacher's desk	
8. The number of cars in the parking lot	
9. The number of tables in the cafeteria	
10. The number of swings on the playground	
11. The width of the classroom door	
12. The number of students with brown hair	
13. The number of steps from the classroom door to the Principal's Office	
14. The time it takes to walk around the school	
15. The time it takes to walk to the library	

Treasure Hunt Worksheet

Instructions for Students: Hunt for the objects listed below. Record your data in the right-hand column.

Look for . . .	*Count . . .*

Evaluating Instruction

Effective teachers continuously monitor their students' understanding of the content being presented. They also monitor their students' use of instructional time to maximize their active engagement in appropriate learning activities. They keep records of progress and use the data to make decisions. In Part IV, we describe evidence-based strategies for each principle of evaluating instruction.

Component	Principle	Strategy
Evaluating Instruction (Part IV)	Monitor Student Understanding (Chapter 10)	Check Understanding of Directions
		Check Procedural Understanding
		Monitor Student Success Rate
	Monitor Engaged Time (Chapter 11)	Check Student Participation/Teach Students to Monitor Their Own Participation
	Keep Records of Student Progress (Chapter 12)	Teach Students to Chart Their Own Progress
		Regularly Inform Students of Performance
		Maintain Records of Student Performance
	Use Data to Make Decisions (Chapter 13)	Use Student Progress to Make Teaching Decisions
		Use Data to Decide If More Services Are Warranted/Use Student Progress to Decide When to Discontinue Services

Evaluating Instruction Works: A Case Study

As a special education teacher who teaches a large number of students with special needs in the general education setting, I am consistently evaluating instruction to provide the appropriate instruction for my students. Although checking for understanding and guiding students to monitor their own participation is crucial, teaching students to maintain and chart their own progress and performance regularly has proven to be a valuable component of my everyday teaching.

I teach my students to maintain their records through weekly progress monitoring probes and assignments. Students record their progress on histograms, pictographs, bar graphs, and in curriculum journals. Students also set goals to maintain a focus on success and achievement. We schedule student-teacher conferences regularly to evaluate student performance and progress. Based on data from student records, we make decisions together either to provide additional services or discontinue services that are no longer needed.

The ultimate goal of evaluating instruction is to provide a means for progressively developing one's independence from teacher-directed learning and advocacy for student-directed learning. Interestingly, in the process of consulting with me, classroom teachers have come to realize that many of the instructional strategies I use are applicable in their instruction—across Tiers I, II, and III. So while my school district does not include students with special needs in Tier III classroom instruction, I've been able to have a wider impact on general education students and, in the process, possibly reduce the number of inappropriate referrals. Also, as general education teachers implement and document their RTI interventions, they are then able to provide evidence in case a special education referral does become necessary.

—*Dustin Mancl*
Elementary School Teacher
Special Education

10

Monitor
Student Understanding

Principle	Strategy
Monitor Student Understanding	Check Understanding of Directions
	Check Procedural Understanding
	Monitor Student Success Rate

Chapter 10: Monitor Student Understanding

Strategy:	**Check Understanding of Directions**

Learning Difference: Seeing; Mobility; Speaking/Talking; Attention

Tactic Title:	**Monitoring Student Understanding in Learning Centers**

Problem:

Teachers often find it difficult to develop lessons that can accommodate diverse learners and enable monitoring of student understanding of directions and procedures.

Tactic:

First, divide students into four groups. Next, assign each group to one of four different reading centers. Each group uses the same book for each reading center.

1. Audio center: Students listen to the book.

2. Teacher center: Teacher reads the book with students.

3. Partner center: Students read the book to each other aloud.

4. Independent center: Students work independently in a journal/illustration book about a topic in the story they have been reading.

Rotate the membership of each group daily so that all students use all four reading centers.

Next, create simple directions (no more than five steps) for students to follow and check off as they complete the work in the center. (Use the Learning Center Checklist on page 132.) Finally, have a representative from each learning center bring the group's checklist to you prior to beginning the activities so that you can clarify any misunderstandings immediately.

Example:

I've used learning centers quite a lot recently and truly believe that they can provide so many additional learning opportunities for my students . . . from remediation to enhancement. However, I will admit that, while learning centers have been proven to be effective, they do take time and careful thought as to their contents and participants. The good news is, I've found that once I've designed a learning center, I can use it over and over again. For example, I have a reading center, a math center, and a creative writing center. I only need to alter the contents to meet the needs of individual students. Keeps me on my toes, and my students love the alternative to just listening to me or working independently all the time.

Tom K., teacher

Benefits:

By including a method for checking student understanding of directions when using learning centers, teachers can

• address the needs of individual students with different learning requirements;

- provide variety and greater interest to students; and
- increase the academic learning time of their students, as well as time for instruction.

RTI Accommodations/Modifications:

Tier I:

- Develop learning centers that address needs for multiple methods of remediation in a content area and incorporate appropriate monitoring activities;
- involve paraprofessionals and other specialists in monitoring student understanding; and/or
- use "clickers" or other technology to check for understanding immediately.

Tier II:

- Create learning centers that require small-group or peer involvement;
- involve peers in monitoring the understanding of directions; and/or
- involve peers in the clarification of directions for others in the center.

Tier III:

- Modify center activities to accommodate individual student needs; and/or
- monitor understanding of directions personally and immediately.

Literature:

Parris, S. R., & Block, C. C. (2007). The expertise of adolescent literacy teachers. *Journal of Adolescent & Adult Literacy, 50,* 582–596.

Schumm, J. S., & Vaughn, S. (1997). How to monitor student understanding in inclusive classrooms. *Intervention in School and Clinic, 32,* 168–171.

Vanderhye, C. M., & Demers, C. (2007–2008). Assessing students' understanding through conversations. *Teaching Children Mathematics, 14,* 260–264.

Learning Center Checklist

Directions:

Teacher: Enter learning center directions in column #1 and student names in row #1. Provide a copy to the lead student in each learning center. Select a lead student in each learning center to be responsible for reviewing directions with peers, obtaining signatures, and delivering signed checklists to you for each learning center immediately. If a student has not signed, provide individual assistance immediately, prior to that student's beginning the activity.

Lead student: Review directions and enter the names of each student in your group in the appropriate box. Then, review activity directions together. Check for understanding with each student. Then, ask each student to sign to indicate that they understand what to do. If some members of your group do not understand, they do not need to sign. Deliver the signed Learning Center Checklist to the teacher prior to beginning any learning center activities.

Center: _____ **Activity:** _____

Directions	Student 1:	Student 2:	Student 3:	Student 4:	Student 5:

Chapter 10: Monitor Student Understanding

Strategy:	**Check Procedural Understanding**

Learning Difference: Cognition Mixed; Attention; Self-control; Memory Short-term; Receptive Language/Decoding (listening, reading); Expressive Language/Encoding (speaking, writing, spelling); Processing Verbal Information

Tactic Title:	**Using Graphic Organizers to Enhance Student Understanding**

Problem: Many students have difficulty remembering instructions and procedures.

Tactic: Use the concepts of main idea and details to practice following expected procedures in a lesson. First, discuss the concept of main idea and details, as well as their relationship to one another. Next, provide an example. For instance, choose the classroom as the main idea and ask the students to pick details (chairs, posters, desks) of the classroom. Then, students fill out a graphic organizer (web) with the main idea as themselves (see Story Web #1 on page 135). Describe the procedures and ask one or two students to repeat the directions aloud. They are to fill in each of the five bubbles with details about themselves. Review their webs by having some students share details and having the class decide if the details are correct. Praise students for following directions and check for understanding again. Distribute the final activity (see Story Web #2 on page 136). Read the directions aloud while students follow along. "A company that makes ice cream has asked us to help. It plans to make an ideal flavor. Any student who can ask 15 questions about this new ice cream flavor will earn a book. Example: Does it have peanuts?" Next, have students work independently and write 7–10 questions about the ice cream. Then, review their questions by having students share their details to be sure that they are grasping the concept of the ice cream being the main idea and their questions being the details. Finally, conclude the activity by recapping the concepts of main idea and details. Ask students to share their thoughts about how they were able to follow directions so well.

Example: I've collaborated with my special education colleague to modify graphic organizers for individual students. For example, some students draw pictures in place of writing words, while others dictate their responses to a peer or paraprofessional. They really understand how to use graphic organizers now, because they practice prior to a lesson when they are with the special education teacher.

Felipe R., teacher

Benefits: Repeating, reviewing, and summarizing procedures

- is applicable across students, content areas, settings, and grade levels;
- enhances student success in completing activities correctly; and
- provides the extra support/scaffolding that some students need.

RTI Accommodations/Modifications:

> *Tier I:*
>
> - Model filling in the graphic organizer with students;
> - verbalize your actions; and/or
> - while recapping, ask students to record their reflections in their journals.
>
> *Tier II:*
>
> - Provide visual and verbal cues;
> - extend time for student responses as needed; and/or
> - list the sequence of activities on the board.
>
> *Tier III:*
>
> - Provide alternative response modes;
> - highlight essential information; and/or
> - provide ongoing supportive/corrective feedback.

Literature:

Ayers, S. F., Housner, L. D., Dietrich, S., Ha Young, K., Pearson, M., Gurvitch, R., et al. (2005). An examination of skill learning using direct instruction. *Physical Educator, 62*, 136–144.

Heller, K. W. (2005). Adaptations and instruction in science and social studies. In S. J. Best, K. W. Heller, & J. L. Bigge (Eds.), *Teaching individuals with physical or multiple disabilities* (5th ed.; pp. 471–499). Upper Saddle River, NJ: Merrill/Prentice Hall.

Penual, W., Boscardin, C., Masyn, K., & Crawford, V. (2007). Teaching with student response systems in elementary and secondary education settings: A survey study. *Educational Technology Research & Development, 55*, 315–346.

Story Web #1

Name _____   **Date**_____

My Classroom

My Classroom

SOURCE: Algozzine, B., Campbell, P., & Wang, A. (2009b). 63 tactics for teaching diverse learners: K–6. Thousand Oaks, CA: Corwin.

Story Web #2

Name _____   **Date**_____

Main Idea/Details

SOURCE: Algozzine, B., Campbell, P., & Wang, A. (2009b). *63 tactics for teaching diverse learners: K–6.* Thousand Oaks, CA: Corwin.

Chapter 10: Monitor Student Understanding

Strategy:	**Monitor Student Success Rate**
Learning Difference:	Receptive Language/Decoding (listening, reading); Expressive Language/Encoding (speaking, writing, spelling)

Tactic Title:	**Monitoring Discrepancies Between Written and Spoken Language**
Problem:	Many students are much more skilled with their written language than they are with their spoken language (and vice versa). It is very important for teachers to be aware of these discrepancies to support the stronger area and address the less skilled aspect of expressive language.
Tactic:	First, review the oral and written language of your students individually. Regarding their oral language, monitor their use of syntax (sentence structure) and grammar (mechanics), phonemes (articulation and pronunciation), morphemes (prefixes, suffixes, word endings), prosody (intonation and inflection), and pragmatics (appropriateness of language given the context). Assess their semantics by examining their vocabulary and comprehension of what they are saying. Regarding their written language, again, monitor their use of syntax (sentence structure) and grammar (mechanics), phonemes (spelling), graphemes (letter formation, spacing, visual representation of information), morphemes (prefixes, suffixes, word endings), pragmatics (appropriateness of language given the genre). Assess their semantics by reviewing the vocabulary used and their level of comprehension (e.g., literal, inferential, predictive). Monitor daily and use your observations and review of written products in your instructional planning.
Example:	I remember Max, a student in my second-grade class several years ago. Did he have me fooled for a while! He'd come in each morning and go to his table, check out the agenda for the day (posted on the board), get his materials ready, and start to do whatever the assigned task was. I have to say that when I'd observed him doing all those things, he kind of fell off my "radar screen" for a bit. Then, one night, when I was trying to fall asleep and was kind of "stewing" as to why his work was so poor, I realized that I ought to be observing him more closely more often. So I made a point of moving around the classroom more and actually seeing what he was doing *and* . . . it was *nothing*! He just "looked good." In addition, he was very fluent and charming verbally . . . . I suddenly realized that he was really struggling to cover up his needs with respect to written language assignments. Needless to say, I changed his instruction immediately, and we started addressing his real needs. Since that time, Max is a different person. He seems much more relaxed and has become a very committed and much more successful learner. I just love it when I finally figure out how to target my teaching appropriately. *Nolan P., teacher*

Benefits: Monitoring possible discrepancies between a student's oral and written
                        language

- is applicable across all grade levels, content areas, and students;
- improves instruction; and
- naturally leads to greater student success.

RTI Accommodations/Modifications:

Tier I:

- Record at least 50 oral student utterances (spoken phrases or sentences) for later review and careful analysis;
- use appropriate questioning to provide opportunities for student success; and/or
- hold regular individual conferences with students to address concerns and celebrate achievements.

Tier II:

- Structure response modes to utilize student strengths in the maintenance and generalization phases of learning (see Table 2 in the Preface);
- structure response modes to provide opportunities to practice and refine student needs in the acquisition and proficiency phases of learning (see Table 2 in the Preface); and/or
- organize students into small groups or dyads to provide models of effective oral and written language for students in need of examples.

Tier III:

- Modify assignment/activity response modes to provide safe opportunities for students to practice needed skills;
- develop learning center activities that target specific skills; and/or
- provide individual instruction.

Literature: Brown, J. E., & Doolittle, J. (2008). A cultural, linguistic, and ecological
                        framework for response to intervention with English language learners.
                        TEACHING Exceptional Children, 40(5), 66–72.

                        Clarke-Klein, S. M. (1994). Expressive phonological deficiencies: Impact
                        on spelling development. *Topics in Language Disorders, 14,* 40.

                        Shafer, G. (1997). Reader response makes history. *English Journal, 86,*
                        65–68.

11

Monitor Engaged Time

Principle	Strategy
Monitor Engaged Time	Check Student Participation/Teach Students to Monitor Their Own Participation

Chapter 11: Monitor Engaged Time

Strategy:	**Check Student Participation/Teach Students to Monitor Their Own Participation**

Learning Difference: Attention; Self-control

Tactic Title:	**Increasing On-Task Behavior by Self-Monitoring**

Problem: Students with attention or emotional issues often find it difficult to concentrate during classroom activities.

Tactic: First, create an audiotape of randomly spaced short tones (from 30 seconds to 5 minutes). Second, generate a simple chart that asks, "Was I paying attention?" and have spaces for students to check yes or no each time the tone sounds. Third, give the chart to the students and explain how to fill in the boxes when they hear the tone. Then, have students record their data on their graph. Lastly, start the audiotape at the beginning of the lesson. Gradually increase time between tones and, as students begin to self-monitor automatically, fade out the use of the tones.

Example: Initially, this tactic was a bit time consuming, but I have found it to be an effective way for individual students to learn to pay attention to their own particular/identified behavior without disrupting other ongoing instruction and learning. While their initial recordings may be "less than accurate," that is not the final goal. First they learn to pay attention to their actions, and then through comparisons with teacher ratings, for example, they learn to be more accurate and thus achieve the original goal. I keep data as well, and we compare my data with the students'. As they have become more and more accurate, we have had more "agreements" than "disagreements." Agreements earn points toward time for a preferred academic computer activity.

Enrico E., teacher

Benefits: Teaching students to self-monitor their own participation

- teaches them a life skill, one that can be used across content areas, grade levels, and contexts;
- reduces interruptions to instruction; and
- increases opportunities for learning for everyone.

RTI Accommodations/Modifications:

Tier I:

- Attach a laminated recording sheet/card to a student's desk or working area;
- seat students who are easily distracted in locations with minimal activity; and/or
- seat students close to you or in a location where you can easily monitor behavior.

Tier II:

- Teach members of small groups/dyads to record one another's on-task behavior;
- provide individual and group rewards for on-task behavior; and/or
- provide modified materials or graphic organizers that remind students to self-monitor at specific times during an activity.

Tier III:

- Modify written materials to include "markers," visual reminders to monitor on-task behavior;
- modify activities to include breaks at specified times during an activity; and/or
- monitor student on-task behavior with the student and compare notes.

Literature:

Baker, S. K., Chard, D. J., Ketterlin-Geller, L. R., Apichatabutra, C., & Doabler, C. (2009). Teaching writing to at-risk students: The quality of evidence for self-regulated strategy development. *Exceptional Children, 75,* 303–318.

Harris, K. R., Friedlander, B. D., Saddler, B., Frizzelle, R., & Graham, S. (2005). Self-monitoring of attention versus self-monitoring of academic performance: Effects among students with ADHD in the general education classroom. *Journal of Special Education, 39*(3), 145–156.

Shimabukuro, S. M., Prater, M. A., Jenkins, A., & Edelen-Smith, P. (1999). The effects of self-monitoring of academic performance on students with learning disabilities and ADD/ADHD. *Education and Treatment of Children, 22,* 397–415.

12

Keep Records
of Student Progress

Principle	Strategy
Keep Records of Student Progress	Teach Students to Chart Their Own Progress
	Regularly Inform Students of Performance
	Maintain Records of Student Performance

Chapter 12: **Keep Records of Student Progress**

Strategy:	**Teach Students to Chart Their Own Progress**

Learning Difference: Self-control; Social Behaviors; Self-confidence; Self-care; Cognition Low; Cognition Mixed; Cognition High; Processing Visual Information; Receptive Language/Decoding (listening, reading); Expressive Language/Encoding (speaking, writing, spelling)

Tactic Title:	**Using Charts to Increase Student Self-Monitoring**

Problem: Maintaining accurate daily records of student achievement can be a time-consuming process for teachers.

Tactic: Use a simple line chart to record student achievement (see Intervention Progress Chart and sample on pages 145 and 146).

1. Select the skill to be measured and enter the learning objective. Include the behavior, student name, measurable action, and the criterion for success, stated either as duration (period of time) or frequency (number of corrects).

2. Enter dates or day # on the horizontal axis and the performance levels on the vertical axis.

3. Enter the baseline data (student performance prior to implementation of the intervention) and draw a vertical line.

4. Enter the data point for reaching the criterion and connect it with baseline date to create the aim line.

5. Enter data points to record performance levels.

Model the charting procedure for students. Provide guided practice to ensure accuracy and consistency.

Example: Over the years, I've collaborated with teachers and specialists from kindergarten through high school, and we've found charting to be a wonderful time-saver. Although it takes little time to teach students how to chart their performance, it really has saved everyone a lot of time. In addition, we have permanent evidence that we can share with parents and other teachers. However, the greatest benefit has been the students' pride in seeing their progress. We've used charting with kindergarteners to record their letter formation accuracy in one-minute timings. We've also taught students in the upper grades to use computer software (spreadsheets, graphs, charts) to record their progress electronically. It really is a tool that can be applied across all grade levels, student abilities, and content area.

Nolan T., learning specialist

Benefits: Charting student performance levels

- motivates students to learn and achieve;
- provides evidence of learning and achievement; and
- can be applied across grade levels, academic content areas, and behavior.

RTI Accommodations/Modifications:

    Tier I:

- Teach students to chart their own progress daily;
- send charts home with students to share data with parents; and
- teach students to share their accomplishments.

    Tiers II and III:

- Use data that indicate students are not making adequate progress and to determine changes to interventions;
- involve students in determining reasons for success or difficulty in learning; and
- adjust the condition, response mode, and/or criterion.

Literature:

Joseph, L. M., & Konrad, M. (2009). Have students self-manage their academic performance. *Intervention in School and Clinic, 44,* 246–249.

Rogers, S., & Renard, L. (1999). Relationship-driven teaching. *Educational Leadership, 57*(1), 34–37.

Intervention Progress Chart

Student Name:_____   Skill to Be Measured:_____

Learning Objective:

Given _____, _____ will _____

        (condition)   (student name)   (measurable action) (frequency/duration)

Intervention:_____

Directions:

1. Enter dates or day #s on the horizontal axis.
2. Enter performance levels on the vertical axis.
3. Enter baseline (starting point) data on the date of the first probe.
4. Draw a vertical line to indicate the end of baseline and the initiation of the intervention.
5. Enter the acceptable performance level on a future date.
6. Connect the data points to create the aim line.
7. Record subsequent probe data in the appropriate place; connect data points to monitor student progress.

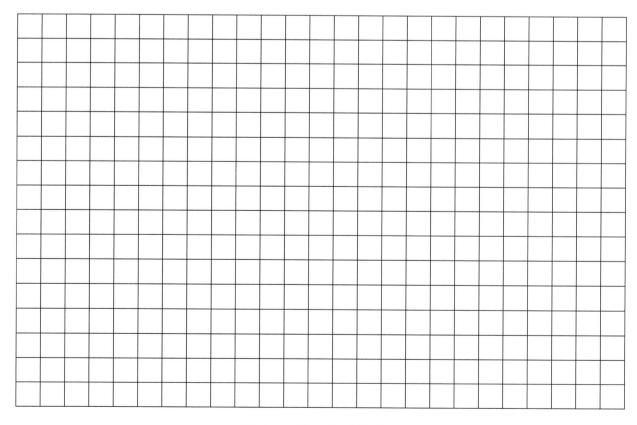

Date or Day # of Probe

Intervention Progress Chart
(Sample)

Student Name: _Sami T._   Skill to be Measured: _Science Vocabulary_

Learning Objective: _(on computer)_
Given _15 science terms_ ‸ , _Sami_ will _match vocabulary words +_
     (condition)   (student name)   (measurable action)   (frequency/duration)

Intervention: _Drill + Practice (computer)_   _definitions with 100% accuracy_

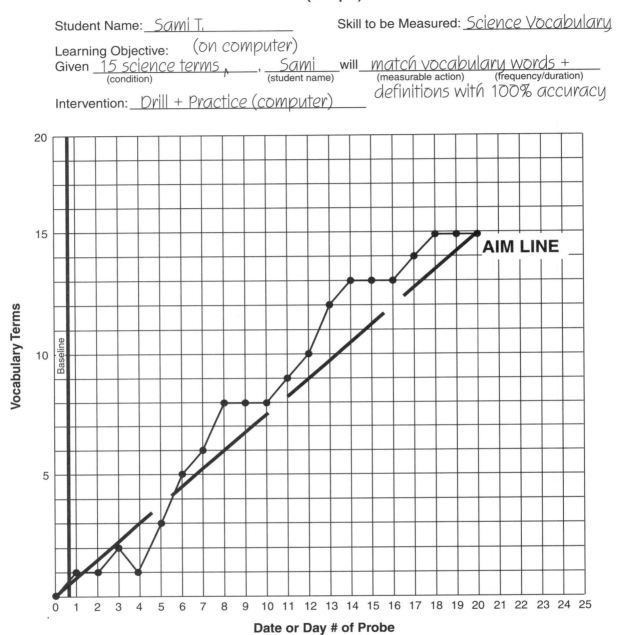

●——● Sami's Performance

Chapter 12: **Keep Records of Student Progress**

Strategy:	Regularly Inform Students of Performance

Learning Difference: Self-control; Social Behaviors; Self-confidence; Self-care; Cognition Low; Cognition Mixed; Cognition High

Tactic Title:	Motivating Students to Learn in a Meaningful Way

Problem: It is difficult to motivate students to learn in all content areas because of individual abilities and interests.

Tactic: To motivate students, use a combination of six guidelines to support relationship-centered teaching and build a motivating learning context:

1. Make students feel safe, physically and emotionally, in your classroom.

2. Provide students with tasks that have value. Students will engage fully and produce quality work if they perceive that what they are doing has value.

3. Show students their progress regularly and in a meaningful way.

4. Involve students in planning and making class decisions about what they are learning.

5. Show students that you care about them and value their opinions. Let students know that they can count on you as a teacher.

6. Constantly seek out the best practices that enable students' learning and ensure that students attain standards.

Example: While these six guidelines may seem very basic, they are actually more complex and challenging to implement on a daily basis—especially with the challenging group of students in my classroom. I keep them in my plan book so I see them every day. Once the students learn that I really do care about them and want them to succeed, they are so motivated to learn. Since I've really focused on implementing these guidelines, the transformation has been amazing.

Shaliah R., teacher

Benefits: Implementing the six guidelines

- motivates students to learn and achieve;
- increases their self-efficacy and self-confidence; and
- provides specific evidence of where they are and what they need to do.

RTI Accommodations/Modifications:

Tier I:

- Teach students to chart their own progress daily;
- provide frequent informative feedback; and/or
- teach students to praise one another.

Tiers II & III:

- Adjust types and amounts of praise and gestures used according to individual student needs/preferences;
- ensure one-on-one interaction with every student; and/or
- teach students to make positive self-statements.

Literature:

Stevens, D. D., & Levi, A. J. (2004). *Introduction to rubrics: An assessment tool to save grading time, convey effective feedback and promote student learning.* Sterling, VA: Stylus.

Twyman, T., & Tindal, G. (2007). Extending curriculum-based measurement into middle/secondary schools: The technical adequacy of the concept maze. *Journal of Applied School Psychology, 24*(1), 49–67.

Chapter 12: **Keep Records of Student Progress**

Strategy:	**Maintain Records of Student Performance**

Learning Difference:	Cognition Mixed; Processing Visual Information; Receptive Language/ Decoding (listening, reading); Expressive Language/Encoding (speaking, writing, spelling)

Tactic Title:	**Using Word Walls to Teach Vocabulary**

Problem:	Even though students may have excellent decoding skills, due to visual memory deficits, they may still have difficulty remembering words that do not follow the "rules."
Tactic:	Words that do not have exact sound/symbol correspondence, such as *what, the, is,* and *to,* can be challenging for some students. These words are commonly referred to as "sight words," "outlaw words," and so forth (depending on the curriculum being used). Students simply have to learn these words and rely on their visual memory or some other "trick" to help them in the beginning. Use a word wall to post these words in alphabetical order so that they are visible throughout the school day. When you are beginning the day's instruction, review the words rapidly using a pointer and choral responding by all students. Then record the number of words that are spoken clearly without delay or error by anyone.
Example:	While this tactic seems "elementary," it really has applications across grade levels, students, and content areas. For example, I teach geometry, and there are many vocabulary words that are unique to my content area and essential for my students to master. So I post these words on a word wall in my classroom, and we review daily, with a twist. When I say a definition, students respond with the word. I've found that this daily fast-paced drill and practice review has helped every single student move through the phases of learning (Acquisition, Proficiency, Maintenance, and Generalization) with great success.

Sylvia S., teacher |
| *Benefits:* | Using, monitoring, and recording student accuracy by using word walls

• builds student vocabulary and is especially important for English-language learners;
• enables teachers to focus on reteaching words that students do not know;
• enhances all aspects of language (oral and written); and
• is applicable across content areas, grade levels, and students. |

RTI Accommodations/Modifications:

Tier I:

- Repeat practice at various times during the school day;
- provide incentives for perfect responding; and/or
- use musical tempos to pace word wall reviews.

Tier II:

- Have students practice word walls in small groups/teams and record results;
- provide copies of word walls for students to practice at home with parents; and/or
- provide incentives for small-group/team achievements.

Tier III:

- Provide individual word walls for students based on their needs;
- tape words to individual word walls for practice throughout the school day and at home; and/or
- involve parents and other teachers in practice opportunities.

Literature:

Jones, E. D., Wilson, R., & Bhojwani, S. (1997). Mathematics instruction for secondary students with learning disabilities. *Journal of Learning Disabilities, 30*(2), 151–163.

Salend, S. (2005). Report card models that support communication and differentiation of instruction. *Teaching Exceptional Children, 37*(4), 28–34.

Shores, C., & Chester, K. (2009). *Using RTI for school improvement: Raising every student's achievement scores.* Thousand Oaks, CA: Corwin.

13

Use Data
to Make Decisions

Chapter 13: Use Data to Make Decisions

Strategy:	**Use Student Progress to Make Teaching Decisions**

Learning Difference: Speaking/Talking; Social Knowledge; Expressive Language/Encoding (speaking, writing, spelling)

Tactic Title:	**Portfolio Assessment**

Problem: Teachers often find it difficult to assess students with diverse abilities in ways that document their achievements, especially when progress is incremental.

Tactic: Portfolios are an effective tool for archiving student work and monitoring student progress over extended periods of time. Students select personally meaningful work to include in their portfolios. Students reflect on why they included the particular pieces and how the selection has affected them as a learner. An ESL student, for example, may show his or her progress through the portfolio without feeling inferior to the rest of the class, who may be working at a more advanced level due to their proficiency with English. Seeing the individual growth of students enables you to make the best instructional decisions.

Example: Portfolios are a wonderful way to assess students who may not be exactly at grade level. They love choosing what to save and write very thoughtful reflections. In fact, this year, we've used student portfolios as as the focus of parent-teacher conferences, which included the students. The students were responsible for reviewing the contents of their portfolios with their parents, talking about their reflections and why they selected items to be included. Most importantly, they were able to talk about their learning and highlight their achievements.

Maurice J., teacher

Benefits: Portfolios help teachers make instructional decisions because they

- illustrate individual progress over time;
- highlight student interests and reflections;
- are developmentally sensitive in that they move with students from year to year and serve as the basis for annual goal setting; and
- afford greater individual flexibility for diverse learners.

RTI Accommodations/Modifications:

Tier I:

- Use electronic portfolios as the tool for teaching students how to upload documents, videos, and podcasts;
- use portfolios to communicate with other educators and parents; and/or
- set aside a time every week for updating portfolios.

Tier II:

- Have students work in small groups or pairs to make decisions about portfolio contents;
- provide a standard format and table of contents for minimal types of materials for portfolios; and/or
- provide models of different portfolios.

Tier III:

- Integrate portfolios into conferences with individual students;
- modify content requirements to highlight individual achievements; and/or
- provide graphic organizers and formats for pages that may be included repeatedly.

Literature:

Algozzine, B., Browder, D., Karvonen, M., Test, D. W., & Wood, W. M. (2001). Effects of interventions to promote self-determination for individuals with disabilities. *Review of Educational Research, 71,* 219–277.

Kleinert, H. L., Browder, D. M., & Towles-Reeves, E. A. (2009). Models of cognition for students with significant cognitive disabilities: Implications for assessment. *Review of Educational Research, 79,* 301–326.

Montgomery, K. (2001). *Authentic assessment: A guide for elementary teachers.* New York: Longman.

Parrish, P. R., & Stodden, R. A. (2009). Aligning assessment and instruction with state standards for children with significant disabilities. *TEACHING Exceptional Children, 41*(4), 46–56.

Chapter 13: Use Data to Make Decisions

Strategy:	**Use Data to Decide If More Services Are Warranted/Use Student Progress to Decide When to Discontinue Services**

Learning Difference:	Cognition Low; Cognition High; Cognition Mixed; Attention; Social Knowledge; Self-control; Receptive Language/Decoding (listening, reading); Expressive Language/Encoding (speaking, writing, spelling); Processing Verbal Information; Social Behaviors; Self-confidence; Self-care; Mobility; Hearing; Health; Memory Short-term; Memory Long-term; Seeing; Speaking/Talking; Study Skills; Fine Motor (handwriting, articulation, etc.); Gross Motor (running, walking, etc.); Processing Visual Information; Processing Verbal Information

Tactic Title:	**Interdisciplinary Daily Teaming**
Problem:	Teachers need time together to assess their students' progress and needs to determine next steps.
Tactic:	To make the best instructional decisions, touch base daily, either in person or electronically, with all teachers (general education teachers, learning specialists, special education teachers, paraprofessionals) involved in your students' education to discuss activities and assignments. Use student self-monitoring data, your own data, and student products to monitor and evaluate student performance and determine whether a more formal meeting is necessary to decide whether to modify a student's program. Focus on both student behaviors and learning needs by looking for patterns in grades, work ethic, and behaviors. Share insights and ideas on how to improve the quality of the team as a whole. Remember to involve parents.
Example:	I teach science in a middle school. Our "Gold Team" meets every day, sometimes in person and often virtually. We include everyone who is involved with our students. Teachers from each of the disciplines, special education, and others (specialists, paraprofessionals, etc.) are included. We use the opportunity to discuss problems with students and possible solutions; also, we remember to celebrate student achievements so that everyone knows and can provide additional support and reinforcement. *Patrick P., teacher*
Benefits:	Daily team meetings ensure • appropriate and timely decisions regarding student programming and services; • coordinated curricula, assignments, and assessments; and • ongoing professional development.

RTI Accommodations/Modifications:

Tiers I, II, & III: Use team meetings as opportunities to

- explore curriculum integration, instructional strategies, goals, and objectives;
- develop common rules, procedures, and monitoring strategies that address individual student needs; and/or
- schedule formal meetings to meet with parents and others regarding modifications to services.

Literature:

Clark, S. N., & Clark, D. N. (1997). Exploring the possibilities of interdisciplinary teaming. *Childhood Education, 73,* 267–271.

Deno, S., & Mirkin, P. (1977). *Data-based program modification.* Minneapolis, MN: Leadership Training Institute for Special Education.

Meltzer, L., & Reid, D. K. (1994). New directions in the assessment of students with special needs: The shift toward a constructivist perspective. *Journal of Special Education, 28,* 338–355.

Wayman, M. M., Wallace, T., Wiley, H. I., Ticha, R., & Espin, C. (2007). Literature synthesis on curriculum-based measurement in reading. *The Journal of Special Education, 41,* 85–120.

RTI Accommodations/ Modifications Checklist

RTI Accommodations/Modifications Checklist

Directions: Use this list of well-known/accepted accommodations as you consider those that might be appropriate for your students. Enter (Tier) I, II, and/or III in the column that relates to the accommodation, as shown in the example. Space has been provided for additions.

	Planning	Managing	Delivering	Evaluating
Example: Pen/pencil grippers			I, II, III	
Books on tape				
Large-print material				
Directions read aloud				
Shortened directions/instructions				
Reduced number of items to be completed				
Fewer items on a single page				
Arrangement of items on a page				
Graph paper for place value				
Guided or class notes to assist in note taking				
Study guide or outline				
Tape recorders to record student content				
Ability to respond orally to content				
Dictation to scribe				
Distraction-free area for working				
Oral testing (individual or tape recorder)				
Oral response (individual or tape recorder)				
Student seated closer to the front or near teacher				
Comprehension check to clarify information				
Preteaching before presenting new material				
Chunking of new information and directions				
Adjustment to length of written assignments				
Allowing extra time to complete work/assessment				
Allowing print, cursive, and/or word processor				
Extra prompts or cues				
Extra textbook for home/school				
Visual reminders				
Marking of due dates on a class calendar				
Manipulatives				
Highlighting important information to cue student				
Rubric				
Recording notes on the progress of each student				
Frequent breaks				
Special lighting				
Pencil grips				
Medium tech (e.g., spell-checker, calculator, etc.)				
Positive reinforcement				
Behavior intervention plan				
Adaptive/special furniture				

	Planning	Managing	Delivering	Evaluating

APPENDIX B

RTI Accommodations/ Modifications Worksheet

RTI Accommodations/Modifications Worksheet

Student Name(s)	Objective(s)	Strength(s)	Need(s)	Task(s)	Accommodation/ Modification

Accommodations/Modifications Worksheet

(sample)

Student Name(s)	Objective(s)	Strength(s)	Need(s)	Task(s)	Accommodation/ Modification
John T.	**Sound/symbol association: Short vowel sounds**	Visual memory	Auditory memory	Name letter sound when given graphic representation of /b/ and /k/.	Provide picture clue (e.g., bat for /b/ or car for /k/).
Elsa F.	**Sound/symbol association: Short vowel sounds**	Auditory memory	Visual memory	Write letter when given sound.	Provide limited printed choices (b/p/d) or (b/x/y) for students to select from and copy.
Manny R.	**Sound/symbol association: Short vowel sounds**	Auditory/ visual memory	Fine motor control	Write letter when sound or graphic representation is provided.	Provide pen/pencil with gripper or computer.
Sophie T.	**States/capitals association**	Visual memory	Auditory memory	Name state capital when given map of state.	Provide graphic reminder with clue, such as a silly sentence: Once I was "lost in" Massachusetts.
Emilio F.	**States/capitals association**	Auditory memory	Visual memory	Name state capital when given name of state.	Provide picture clue that rhymes or starts with name or beginning sound of state capital (e.g., "Lost in" space or "**Baked Beans**") on map of state.
Juan-Ju W.	**States/capitals association**	Auditory/ visual memory	Fine motor control	Name state capital when given name of state.	Provide pen/pencil with gripper or computer.
Susanna T.	**Political process**	Cognitive abilities	Social competence	Write original essay defending our political process.	Assign cooperative learning role of Group Organizer— responsible for group's success in collaborating.
Allendo F.	**Political process**	Ability to follow directions/ Motivation	Cognitive abilities	Write original essay defending our political process.	Assign cooperative learning role of Timekeeper/ Materials Organizer.

APPENDIX C

Documentation of RTI Accommodations/ Modifications

Documentation of **RTI** Accommodations/Modifications

Student Name:_____   **Tier: I   II   III**

Content Area:_____

RTI Modifications	Start Date	Observations	Evidence	End Date

References

Adams, G. L., & Engelmann, S. (1996). *Research on direct instruction: 25 years beyond DISTAR*. Seattle: Educational Achievement Systems.

Adamson, H. (1993). *Academic competence*. New York: Longman.

Akande, A. (1997). The role of reinforcement in self-monitoring. *Education, 118,* 275.

Algozzine, B., Browder, D., Karvonen, M., Test, D. W., & Wood, W. M. (2001). Effects of interventions to promote self-determination for individuals with disabilities. *Review of Educational Research, 71,* 219–277.

Algozzine, B., Campbell, P., & Wang, A. (2009a). *63 tactics for teaching diverse learners: Grades 6–12*. Thousand Oaks, CA: Corwin.

Algozzine, B., Campbell, P., & Wang, A. (2009b). *63 tactics for teaching diverse learners: K–6*. Thousand Oaks, CA: Corwin.

Algozzine, B., & Ysseldyke, J. E. (1992). *Strategies and tactics for effective instruction*. Longmont, CO: Sopris West.

Algozzine, B., Ysseldyke, J., & Elliott, J. (1997). *Strategies and tactics for effective instruction*. Longmont, CO: Sopris West.

Allsopp, D. H. (1997). Using classwide peer tutoring to teach beginning algebra problem-solving skills in heterogeneous classrooms. *Remedial and Special Education, 18,* 367–379.

Anderson, L. W., & Krathwohl, D. R. (Eds.). (2001). *A taxonomy for learning, teaching, and assessing: A revision of Bloom's taxonomy of educational objectives* (abridged). New York: Longman.

Applebaum, M. (2009). *The one-stop guide to implementing RTI: Academic and behavioral interventions, K–12*. Thousand Oaks, CA: Corwin.

Ayers, S. F., Housner, L. D., Dietrich, S., Ha Young, K., Pearson, M., Gurvitch, R., et al. (2005). An examination of skill learning using direct instruction. *Physical Educator, 62,* 136–144.

Baker, S. K., Chard, D. J., Ketterlin-Geller, L. R., Apichatabutra, C., & Doabler, C. (2009). Teaching writing to at-risk students: The quality of evidence for self-regulated strategy development. *Exceptional Children, 75,* 303–318.

Banda, D. R., Grimmett, E., & Hart, S. L. (2009). Activity schedules: Helping students with autism spectrum disorders in general education classrooms manage transition issues. *TEACHING Exceptional Children, 41*(4), 16–21.

Bender, W. N. (2009). *Differentiating math instruction: Strategies that work for K–8 classrooms* (2nd ed.). Thousand Oaks, CA: Corwin.

Bender, W. N., & Larkin, M. J. (2009). *Reading strategies for elementary students with learning difficulties: Strategies for RTI*. Thousand Oaks, CA: Corwin.

Boulineau, T., Fore, C., III, Hagan-Burke, S., & Burke, M. D. (2004). Use of story-mapping to increase the story-grammar text comprehension of elementary students with learning disabilities. *Learning Disability Quarterly, 27,* 105–120.

Box, J. A., & Little, D. C. (2003). Cooperative small-group instruction combined with advance organizers and their relationship to self-concept and social studies achievement of elementary school students. *Journal of Instructional Psychology, 30,* 285–287.

Bradley, R., Danielson, L., & Doolittle, J. (2007). Responsiveness to intervention: 1997 to 2007. *TEACHING Exceptional Children, 39*(5), 8–12.

Brown, J. E., & Doolittle, J. (2008). A cultural, linguistic, and ecological framework for response to intervention with English language learners. *TEACHING Exceptional Children, 40*(5), 66–72.

Calhoun, M. B., Otaiba, S. A., Cihak, D., King, A., & Avalos, A. (2007). Effects of a peer-mediated program on reading skill acquisition for two-way bilingual first-grade classrooms. *Learning Disability Quarterly, 30,* 169–180.

Campbell, P., & Siperstein, G. P. (1994). *Developing social competence: A resource for elementary teachers.* Boston: Allyn & Bacon.

Carnine, D. W., Silbert, J., Kame'enui, E. F., & Tarver, S. G. (2004). *Direct instruction reading* (4th ed.). Upper Saddle River, NJ: Pearson/Merrill Prentice Hall.

Castagno, A. E., & Brayboy, B. M. J. (2008). Culturally responsive schooling for indigenous youth: A review of the literature. *Review of Educational Research, 78,* 941–993.

CEC's policy on safe and positive school climate. (2008). *TEACHING Exceptional Children, 40*(60), 41–42.

Chorzempa, B. F., & Lapidus, L. (2009). "To find yourself, think for yourself": Using Socratic discussions in inclusive classrooms. *TEACHING Exceptional Children, 41*(3), 54–59.

Christensen, L., Young, K. R., & Marchant, M. (2004). The effects of a peer-mediated positive behavior support program on socially appropriate classroom behavior. *Education and Treatment of Children, 27,* 199–234.

Clark, S. N., & Clark, D. N. (1997). Exploring the possibilities of interdisciplinary teaming. *Childhood Education, 73,* 267–271.

Clarke-Klein, S. M. (1994). Expressive phonological deficiencies: Impact on spelling development. *Topics in Language Disorders, 14,* 40.

Conroy, M. A., Sutherland, K. S., Snyder, A. L., & Marsh, S. (2008). Classwide interventions: Effective instruction makes a difference. *TEACHING Exceptional Children, 40*(6), 24–30.

Cunningham, M., Corprew, C. S., III, & Becker, J. E. (2009). Associations of future expectations, negative friends, and academic achievement in high-achieving African American adolescents. *Urban Education, 44,* 280–296.

Davis, G. N., Lindo, E. J., & Compton, D. L. (2007). Using graphic organizers to attain relational knowledge from expository text. *Journal of Learning Disabilities, 35,* 306–320.

Deno, S., & Mirkin, P. (1977). *Data-based program modification.* Minneapolis, MN: Leadership Training Institute for Special Education.

Deshler, D. D., Ellis, E. S., & Lenz, B. K. (1996). *Teaching adolescents with learning disabilities* (2nd ed.). Denver: Love.

Deshler, D. D., Schumaker, J. B., & Woodruff, S. K. (2004). Improving literacy skills of at-risk adolescents: A schoolwide response. In D. S. Strickland & D. E. Alvermann (Eds.), *Bridging the literacy achievement gap grades 4–12* (pp. 86–106). New York: Teachers College Press.

Díaz-Rico, L. T., & Weed, K. Z. (in press). *The crosscultural, language, and academic handbook: A complete K–12 reference guide* (4th ed.). Boston: Allyn & Bacon/Pearson.

Din, F. S., Isack, L. R., & Rietveld, J. (2003, February–March). *Effects of contingency contracting on decreasing student tardiness.* Paper presented at the annual conference of the Eastern Educational Research Association, Hilton Head Island, SC.

Dolan, R. P., Hall, T. E., Banerjee, M., Chun, E., & Strangman, N. (2005). Applying principles of universal design to test delivery: The effect of computer-based read-aloud on test performance of high school students with learning disabilities. *Journal of Technology, Learning, and Assessment, 3*(7). Available May 6, 2009, at http://escholarship.bc.edu/jtla/.

Dollard, N. (1996). Constructive classroom management. *Focus on Exceptional Children, 29,* 1–12.

DuPaul, G. J., Gardill, M. C., & Kyle, K. E. (1996). Classroom strategies for managing students with ADHD. *Intervention in School and Clinic, 32,* 89–94.

DuPaul, G. J., & Kyle, K. E. (1996). Classroom strategies for managing students with ADHD. *Intervention in school and clinic, 32,* 318–319.

Dyson, B. J. (2008). Assessing small-scale interventions in large-scale teaching: A general methodology and preliminary data. *Active Learning in Higher Education, 9,* 265–282.

Eber, L., Breen, K., Rose, J., Unizycki, R. M., & London, T. (2008). Wraparound as a tertiary-level intervention for students with emotional/behavioral needs. *TEACHING Exceptional Children, 40*(6), 16–22.

Echevarria, J., Short, D., & Powers, K. (2006). School reform and standards-based education: A model for English-language learners. *The Journal of Educational Research, 99*, 195–210.

Ehri, L. C., Nunes, S. R., Stahl, S. A., & Willows, D. M. (2001). Systematic phonics instruction helps students learn to read: Evidence from the National Reading Panel's meta-analysis. *Review of Educational Research, 71*(3), 393–447.

Ellis, E. S., & Worthington, L. A. (1994). *Research synthesis on effective teaching principles and the design of quality tools for educators* (Technical Report No. 5). Eugene: University of Oregon, National Center to Improve the Tools of Educators. (ERIC Document Reproduction Service No. ED386853)

Ellsworth, J. (1996). Enhancing student responsibility to increase student success. *Educational Horizons, 76*, 17–22.

Epstein, M., Polloway, E., Buck, G., Bursuck, W., Wissinger, L., Whitehouse, F., et al. (1997). Homework-related communication problems: Perspectives of general education teachers. *Learning Disabilities Research and Practice, 12*, 221–227.

Fachin, K. (1996). Teaching Tommy: A second grader with attention deficit hyperactivity disorder. *Phi Delta Kappan, 77*, 437–441.

Fairbanks, S., Simonsen, B., & Sugai, G. (2008). Classwide secondary and tertiary tier practices and systems. *TEACHING Exceptional Children, 40*(6), 44–52.

Fore, C., III, Riser, S., & Boon, R. (2006). Implications of cooperative learning and educational reform for students with mild disabilities. *Reading Improvement, 43*(1), 3–12.

Foster, K. C. (2008). The transformative potential of teacher care as described by students in a higher education access initiative. *Education and Urban Society, 41*(1), 104–126.

Fuchs, D., & Deshler, D. D. (2007). What we need to know about responsiveness to intervention (and shouldn't be afraid to ask). *Learning Disabilities Research & Practice, 22*, 129–136.

Fuchs, L. S., & Fuchs, D. (2007). A model for implementing responsiveness to intervention. *TEACHING Exceptional Children, 39*(5), 12–20.

Fulk, D. J., & Montgomery-Grymes, D. J. (1994). Strategies to improve student motivation. *Intervention in School and Clinic, 30*, 28–33.

Gable, R. A., Hester, P. H., Rock, M. L., & Hughes, K. G. (2009). Back to basics: Rules, praise, ignoring, and reprimands revisited. *Intervention in School and Clinic, 44*, 195–205.

Gardner, H. (1999). *Intelligence reframed: Multiple intelligences for the 21st century.* New York: Basic Books.

Garza, R. (2009). Latino and White high school students' perceptions of caring behaviors: Are we culturally responsive to our students? *Urban Education, 44*, 237–321.

Gentry, M., Hu, S., Peters, S. J., & Rizza, M. (2008). Talented students in an exemplary career and technical education school: A qualitative inquiry. *Gifted Child Quarterly, 52*, 183–198.

Golick, M. (1985). *Deal me in.* New York: Norton.

Goodlad, J. (2000). Education and democracy: Advancing the agenda. *Phi Delta Kappan, 82*(1), 86–89.

Graham, S., Morphy, P., Harris, K. R., Fink-Chorzempa, B., Saddler, B., Moran, S., et al. (2008). Teaching spelling in the primary grades: A national survey of instructional practices and adaptations. *American Educational Research Journal, 45*, 796–825.

Greenwood, C. R., Horton, B. T., & Utley, C. A. (2002). Academic engagement: Current perspectives in research and practice. *School Psychology Review, 31*, 328–349.

Griffiths, A.-M., VanDerHeyden, A. M., Parson, L. B., & Burns, M. K. (2008). Examination of the utility of various measures of mathematics proficiency. *Learning Disabilities, 34*, 34–58.

Guernsey, M. A. (1989). Classroom organization: A key to successful management. *Academic Therapy, 25*, 55–58.

Hall, S. L. (2008). *Implementing response to intervention.* Thousand Oaks, CA: Corwin.

Harris, K. R., Friedlander, B. D., Saddler, B., Frizzelle, R., & Graham, S. (2005). Self-monitoring of attention versus self-monitoring of academic performance: Effects among students with ADHD in the general education classroom. *Journal of Special Education, 39*(3), 145–156.

Hattie, J., & Timperley, H. (2007). The power of feedback. *Review of Educational Research, 77*, 81–112.

Heller, K. W. (2005). Adaptations and instruction in science and social studies. In S. J. Best, K. W. Heller, & J. L. Bigge (Eds.), *Teaching individuals with physical or multiple disabilities* (5th ed.; pp. 471–499). Upper Saddle River, NJ: Merrill/Prentice Hall.

Hoover, J. J. (2009). *RTI: Assessment essentials for struggling learners.* Thousand Oaks, CA: Corwin.

Huang, E. (2009). Teaching button-pushing versus teaching thinking: The state of new media education in U.S. universities. *Convergence, 15,* 233–247.

Hudson, P. (1997). Using teacher-guided practice to help students with learning disabilities acquire and retain social studies content. *Learning Disabilities Quarterly, 20,* 23–32.

Hudson, P., Miller, S., & Butler, F. (2006). Integrating reform-based mathematics and explicit teaching in inclusive classrooms. *American Secondary Education, 35,* 19–32.

Hughes, T. A., & Fredrick, L. D. (2006). Teaching vocabulary with students with learning disabilities using classwide peer tutoring and constant time delay. *Journal of Behavioral Education, 15,* 1–23.

Hurd, D. W. (1997). Novelty and its relation to field trips. *Education/Print Source Plus, 118,* 29–35.

Jenkins, J. R., Antil, L. R., Wayne, S. K., & Vadasy, P. F. (2003). How cooperative learning works for special education and remedial students. *Exceptional Children, 69,* 279–292.

Jitendra, A. K., Deatline-Buchman, A., & Sczesniak, E. (2005). A comparative analysis of third-grade mathematics textbooks before and after the 2000 NCTM standards. *Effective Intervention, 30,* 47–62.

Jones, E. D., Wilson, R., & Bhojwani, S. (1997). Mathematics instruction for secondary students with learning disabilities. *Journal of Learning Disabilities, 30*(2), 151–163.

Joseph, L. M., & Konrad, M. (2009). Have students self-manage their academic performance. *Intervention in School and Clinic, 44,* 246–249.

Jung, L. A., Gomez, C., Baird, S. M., & Gaylon Keramidas, C. L. (2008). Designing intervention plans: Bridging the gap between individualized education programs and implementation. *TEACHING Exceptional Children, 41*(1), 26–33.

Kemp, K., Fister, S., & McLaughlin, P. J. (1995). Academic strategies for children with ADD. *Intervention in School and Clinic, 30,* 203–210.

Kerr, M. M., & Nelson, C. M. (2006). *Strategies for managing behavior problems in the classroom* (5th ed.). Upper Saddle River, NH: Merrill/Prentice Hall.

King-Sears, M. E. (2007). Designing and delivering learning center instruction. *Intervention in School and Clinic, 42,* 137–147.

Kleinert, H. L., Browder, D. M., & Towles-Reeves, E. A. (2009). Models of cognition for students with significant cognitive disabilities: Implications for assessment. *Review of Educational Research, 79,* 301–326.

Konrad, M., Helf, S., & Itoi, M. (2007). More bang for the book: Using children's literature to promote self-determination and literacy skills. *TEACHING Exceptional Children, 40*(1), 64–71.

Kroesbergen, E. H., Van Luit, J. E. H., & Maas, C. J. M. (2004). Effectiveness of explicit and constructivist mathematics instruction for low-achieving students in the Netherlands. *Elementary School Journal, 104,* 233–251.

Kucan, L., & Beck, I. L. (1997). Thinking aloud and reading comprehension research: Inquiry, instruction, and social interaction. *Review of Educational Research, 67,* 271–299.

Lacourse, M. (1997). A plan to reduce transition time in physical education. *Journal of Physical Education, Recreation & Dance, 68,* 30.

Lance, D. M., Beverly, B. L., Evans, L. H., & McCullough, K. C. (2003). Addressing literacy: Effective methods for reading instruction. *Communication Disorders Quarterly, 25,* 5–11.

Lassen, S. R., Steele, M. M., & Sailor, W. (2006). The relationship of schoolwide positive behavior support to academic achievement in an urban middle school. *Psychology in the School, 43,* 701–712.

Lee, D. L. (2006). Facilitating transitions between and within academic tasks. *Remedial and Special Education, 27,* 312–317.

Lee, S.-H., Palmer, S. B., & Wehmeyer, M. L. (2009). Goal setting and self-monitoring for students with disabilities: Practical tips and ideas for teachers. *Intervention in School and Clinic, 44,* 139–145.

Lee, S.-H., Soukup, J. H., Little, T. D., & Wehmeyer, M. L. (2009). Student and teacher variables contributing to access to the general education curriculum for students with intellectual and developmental disabilities. *The Journal of Special Education, 43*(1), 29–44.

Madsen, C. H., Jr., Becker, C. W., & Thomas, D. R. (2001). Rules, praise, and ignoring: Elements of elementary classroom control. *Journal of Direct Instruction, 1*(1), 11–25.

Martinez-Roldan, C. M., & Lopez-Robertson, J. M. (2000). Initiating literature circles in a first-grade bilingual classroom. *The Reading Teacher, 53,* 270–281.

Marzano, R. J. (2003). *Classroom management that works: Research-based strategies for every teacher.* Alexandria, VA: Association for Supervision and Curriculum Development.

Marzano, R. J., Pickering, D. J., & Pollack, J. E. (2001). *Classroom instruction that works: Research-based strategies for increasing student achievement.* Alexandria, VA: Association for Supervision and Curriculum Development.

Mastropieri, M. A., & Scruggs, T. E. (1998). Enhancing school success with mnemonic strategies. *Intervention in School and Clinic, 33,* 201–208.

Mastropieri, M. A., Scruggs, T. E., & Bohs, K. (1994). Mainstreaming an emotionally handicapped student in science: A qualitative investigation. In T. E. Scruggs & M. A. Mastropieri (Eds.), *Advances in learning and behavioral disabilities* (Vol. 8; pp. 131–146). Greenwich, CT: JAI.

Mastropieri, M. A., Scruggs, T. E., & Cicciarelli, S. (2007, April). *Overcoming a significant challenge: Motivating students to learn!* Paper presented at the annual meeting of the Council for Exceptional Children, Louisville, KY.

Mastropieri, M. A., Scruggs, T. E., Norland, J. J., Berkeley, S., McDuffie, K., Tornquist, E. H., et al. (2006). Differentiated curriculum enhancement in inclusive middle school science: Effects on classroom and high-stakes tests. *The Journal of Special Education, 40,* 130–137.

Mazur, K. (2004). An introduction to inclusion in the music classroom. *General Music Today, 18,* 6–11.

McLeod, V. (1987). The teaching of music to primary children in schools for the visually handicapped compared with mainstream schools. *British Journal of Visual Impairment, 5,* 99–101.

McNeely, C. A., Nonnemaker, J. M., & Blum, R. W. (2002). Promoting school connectedness: Evidence from the National Longitudinal Study of Adolescent Health. *Journal of School Health, 72*(4), 138–146.

Meadan, H., & Monda-Amaya, L. (2008). Collaboration to promote social competence for students with mild disabilities in the general classroom: A structure for providing social support. *Intervention in School and Clinic, 43,* 158–167.

Mechling, L. C. (2007). Assistive technology as a self-management tool for prompting students with intellectual disabilities to initiate and complete daily tasks: A literature review. *Education and Training in Development Disabilities, 42,* 252–269.

Mellard, D. F., & Johnson, E. (2008). *RTI: A practitioner's guide to implementing response to intervention.* Thousand Oaks, CA: Corwin.

Meltzer, L., & Reid, D. K. (1994). New directions in the assessment of students with special needs: The shift toward a constructivist perspective. *Journal of Special Education, 28,* 338–355.

Mercer, C. D., & Mercer, A. R. (2005). *Teaching students with learning problems* (7th ed.). Columbus, OH: Merrill/Prentice Hall.

Mettas, A., & Constantinou, C. (2008). The technology fair: A project-based learning approach for enhancing problem-solving skills and interest in design and technology education. *Journal of Technology and Design Education, 18*(1), 79–100.

Miller, S. P. (2009). *Validated practices for teaching students with diverse needs and abilities* (2nd ed.). Upper Saddle River, NJ: Pearson/Merrill.

Miller, S. P., & Hudson, P. J. (2007). Using evidence-based practices to build mathematics competence related to conceptual, procedural, and declarative knowledge. *Learning Disabilities Research & Practice, 22,* 47–57.

Montgomery, K. (2001). *Authentic assessment: A guide for elementary teachers.* New York: Longman.

Mooney, P., Ryan, J. B., Uhing, B. M., Reid, R., & Epstein, M. H. (2005). A review of self-management interventions targeting academic outcomes for students with emotional and behavioral disorders. *Journal of Behavioral Education, 14,* 203–221.

More, C. (2009). Digital stories targeting social skills for children with disabilities: Multidimensional learning. *Intervention in School and Clinic, 43,* 168–177.

Morgan, M., & Moni, K. B. (2007). Motivate students with disabilities using sight-vocabulary activities. *Intervention in School & Clinic, 4,* 229–233.

Mullins, D. (1996). A quartet of success stories: How to make inclusion work. *Educational Leadership, 53,* 51–55.

Murphy, D. M. (1996). Implications of inclusion for general and special education. *The Elementary School Journal, 96,* 469–493.

National Institute of Child Health and Human Development Early Child Care Research Network. (2005). A day in third grade: A large-scale study of classroom quality and teacher and student behavior. *Elementary School Journal, 105,* 305–323.

Nelson, J. S., Jayanthi, M., Epstein, M. H., & Bursuck, W. D. (2000). Student preferences for adaptations in classroom testing. *Remedial and Special Education, 21,* 41–52.

Noddings, N. (2005). *The challenge to care in schools: An alternative approach to education* (2nd ed.). New York: Teachers College Press.

Oortwijn, M. B., Boekaerts, M., & Vedder, P. (2008). The impact of a cooperative learning experience on pupils' popularity, non-cooperativeness, and interethnic bias in multiethnic elementary schools. *Educational Psychology, 28*(2), 1–11.

Osburn, H. (2006). Creativity and planning: Training interventions to develop creative problem-solving skills. *Creativity Research Journal, 18,* 173–190.

Osterman, K. F. (2000). Students' need for belonging in the school community. *Review of Educational Research, 70,* 323–367.

Oswald, K., Safran, S., & Johanson, G. (2005). Preventing trouble: Making schools safer places using positive behavior supports. *Education and Treatment of Children, 28,* 265–278.

Parris, S. R., & Block, C. C. (2007). The expertise of adolescent literacy teachers. *Journal of Adolescent & Adult Literacy, 50,* 582–596.

Parrish, P. R., & Stodden, R. A. (2009). Aligning assessment and instruction with state standards for children with significant disabilities. *TEACHING Exceptional Children, 41*(4), 46–56.

Pearl, C. (2009). Laying the foundation for self-advocacy: Fourth graders with learning disabilities invite their peers into the resource room. *TEACHING Exceptional Children, 36*(3), 44–49.

Penual, W., Boscardin, C., Masyn, K., & Crawford, V. (2007). Teaching with student response systems in elementary and secondary education settings: A survey study. *Educational Technology Research & Development, 55,* 315–346.

Perone, V. (1994). How to engage students in learning. *Educational Leadership, 52*(5), 11–13.

Peterson-Miller, S. (1996). Promoting strategic math performance to students with learning disabilities. *Learning Disabilities Forum, 21,* 34–40.

Pianta, R. C., Belsky, J., Vandergrift, N., Houts, R., & Morrison, F. J. (2008). Classroom effects on children's achievement trajectories in elementary school. *American Educational Research Journal, 45,* 365–397.

Rademacher, J. A., Shumaker, J. B., & Deshler, D. D. (1996). Development and validation of a classroom assignment routine for inclusive settings. *Learning Disability Quarterly, 19,* 163–177.

Reid, R., Trout, A. L., & Schartz, M. (2005). Self-regulation interventions for children with attention deficit/hyperactivity disorder. *Exceptional Children, 71,* 361–377.

Renzulli, J. S., & Reis, S. M. (2002). What is schoolwide enrichment and how do gifted programs relate to total school improvement? *Gifted Child Today, 25*(4), 18–25.

Ridling, Z. (1994, April). *The effects of three seating arrangements on teachers' use of selective interactive verbal behaviors.* Paper presented at the annual meeting of the American Educational Research Association, New Orleans, LA.

Rief, S. F. (1993). *How to reach and teach ADD/ADHD children.* West Nyack, NY: Center for Applied Research in Education.

Rock, M. L., & Thead, B. K. (2009). Promote student success during independent seatwork. *Intervention in School and Clinic, 44,* 179–184.

Rogers, S., & Renard, L. (1999). Relationship-driven teaching. *Educational Leadership, 57*(1), 34–37.

Rosenberg, M. S., & Jackman, L. A. (2003). Development, implementation, and sustainability of comprehensive schoolwide behavior management systems. *Intervention in School and Clinic, 39,* 10–21.

Rosenshine, B., & Stevens, R. (1986). Teaching functions. In M. C. Wittrock (Ed.), *Handbook of research on teaching* (3rd ed.; pp. 376–391). New York: Macmillan.

Rothstein-Fisch, C., Greenfield, P. M., & Trumbull, E. (1999). Bridging cultures with classroom strategies. *Educational Leadership, 56,* 64–67.

Rowe, M. B. (1986). Wait time: Slowing down may be a way of speeding up! *Journal of Teacher Education, 37,* 43–50.

Saenz, L. M., Fuchs, L. S., & Fuchs, D. (2005). Peer-assisted learning strategies for English language learners with learning disabilities. *Exceptional Children, 71,* 231–247.

Salend, S. (2005). Report card models that support communication and differentiation of instruction. *TEACHING Exceptional Children, 37*(4), 28–34.

Salend, S. (2008). *Creating inclusive classrooms: Effective and reflective practices* (6th ed.). Upper Saddle River, NJ: Merrill/Prentice Hall.

Schlichter, C. L. (1986). An inservice education model for teaching thinking skills. *Gifted Child Quarterly, 30,* 119–123.

Schnakenberg, J. W. (2009). A synthesis of reading interventions and effects on reading comprehension outcomes for older struggling readers. *Review of Educational Research, 79,* 262–300.

Schumm, J. S., & Vaughn, S. (1997). How to monitor student understanding in inclusive classrooms. *Intervention in School & Clinic, 32,* 168–171.

Schumm, J. S., Vaughn, S., Haager, D., McDowell, J., Rothlein, L., & Saumell, L. (1995). General education teacher planning: What can students with learning disabilities expect? *Exceptional Children, 61,* 335–352.

Schumm, J. S., Vaughn, S., & Leavell, A. G. (1994). Planning pyramid: A framework for planning for diverse student needs during content area instruction. *The Reading Teacher, 47,* 608–615.

Seo, S., Brownell, M. T., Bishop, A. G., & Dingle, M. (2008). An examination of beginning special education teachers' classroom practices that engage elementary students with learning disabilities in reading instruction. *Exceptional Children, 75,* 97–122.

Shafer, G. (1997). Reader response makes history. *English Journal, 86,* 65–68.

Shimabukuro, S. M., Prater, M. A., Jenkins, A., & Edelen-Smith, P. (1999). The effects of self-monitoring of academic performance on students with learning disabilities and ADD/ADHD. *Education and Treatment of Children, 22,* 397–415.

Shores, C. (2009). *A comprehensive RTI model: Integrating behavioral and academic interventions.* Thousand Oaks, CA: Corwin.

Shores, C., & Chester, K. (2009). *Using RTI for school improvement: Raising every student's achievement scores.* Thousand Oaks, CA: Corwin.

Simmons, D. C., Fuchs, D., & Fuchs, L. S. (1991). Instructional and curricular requisites of mainstreamed students with learning disabilities. *Journal of Learning Disabilities, 24,* 354–360.

Simonsen, B., Sugai, G., & Negron, M. (2008). Schoolwide positive behavior supports: Primary systems and practices. *TEACHING Exceptional Children, 40*(6), 32–40.

Slavin, R. E. (2000). *Cooperative learning: Theory, research and practice* (2nd ed.). Boston: Allyn & Bacon.

Soder, R. (1995). *Democracy, education, and the schools.* San Francisco: Jossey-Bass.

Soder, R., Goodlad, J. I., & McMannon, T. J. (2001). *Developing democratic character in the young.* San Francisco: Jossey-Bass.

Stecker, P. M., Whinnery, K. Q., & Duxh, L. A. (1996). Self-recording during unsupervised academic activity: Effects on time spent out of class. *Exceptionality, 6,* 133–147.

Stevens, D. D., & Levi, A. J. (2004). Introduction to rubrics: An assessment tool to save grading time, convey effective feedback and promote student learning. Sterling, VA: Stylus.

Sugai, G. (2005, November). *Establishing a continuum of support inside the classroom.* Paper presented at the annual Making Connections Conference, Vancouver, BC, Canada.

Sugai, G. (2008). *School-wide positive behavior support and response to intervention.* Retrieved April 9, 2009, from http://www.rtinetwork.org

Swinson, J., & Knight, R. (2007). Teacher verbal feedback directed towards secondary pupils with challenging behaviour and its relationship to their behaviour. *Educational Psychology in Practice, 23,* 241–255.

Tomlinson, C. A. (2004). *The differentiated classroom: Responding to the needs of all learners.* Upper Saddle River, NJ: Prentice-Hall.

Twyman, T., & Tindal, G. (2007). Extending curriculum-based measurement into middle/secondary schools: The technical adequacy of the concept maze. *Journal of Applied School Psychology, 24*(1), 49–67.

U. S. Department of Education: Assistance to States for the Education of Children with Disabilities and Preschool Grants for Children with Disabilities; Final Rule. 34 C.F.R. pts. 300–301 (2006). Printing in 71 Fed Reg. 46,540–46,845 (Aug. 14, 2006) available May 6, 2009, at http://idea.ed.gov/download/finalregulations.pdf

Uberti, H. Z., Scruggs, T. E., & Mastropieri, M. A. (2003). Keywords make the difference! Mnemonic instruction in inclusive classrooms. *TEACHING Exceptional Children, 35*(3), 57–61.

Vaidya, S. R. (1999). Metacognitive learning strategies for students with learning disabilities. *Education, 120,* 186–189.

Vallecorsa, A. L., & deBettencourt, L. U. (1997). Using a mapping procedure to teach reading and writing skills to middle grade students with learning disabilities. *Education and Treatment of Children, 20,* 173–188.

Vanderhye, C. M., & Demers, C. (2007–2008). Assessing students' understanding through conversations. *Teaching Children Mathematics, 14,* 260–264.

Veerkamp, M. B., Kamps, D. M., & Cooper, L. (2007). The effects of classwide peer tutoring on the reading achievement of urban middle school students. *Education and Treatment of Children, 30*(2), 21–51.

Walsh, J. M. (2001). Getting the "big picture" of IEP goals and state standards. *TEACHING Exceptional Children, 33*(5), 18–26.

Walshaw, M., & Anthony, G. (2008). The teacher's role in classroom discourse: A review of recent research into mathematics classrooms. *Review of Educational Research, 78,* 516–551.

Wang, M. C., Haertel, G. D., & Walberg, H. J. (1993). Toward a knowledge base for school learning. *Review of Educational Research, 63,* 249–294.

Wanzek, J., Vaughn, S., Wexler, J., Swanson, E. A., Edmonds, M., & Kim, A. (2006). A synthesis of spelling and reading interventions and their effects on the spelling outcomes of students with LD. *Journal of Learning Disabilities, 39,* 528–543.

Wayman, M. M., Wallace, T., Wiley, H. I., Ticha, R., & Espin, C. (2007). Literature synthesis on curriculum-based measurement in reading. *The Journal of Special Education, 41,* 85–120.

Werts, M. G., Caldwell, N. K., & Wolery, M. (2003). Instructive feedback: Effects of a presentation variable. *Journal of Special Education, 37,* 124–133.

Wilkinson, L. A. (2003). Using behavioral consultation to reduce challenging behavior in the classroom. *Preventing School Failure, 47*(3), 100–105.

Wolford, P. L., Heward, W. L., & Alber, S. R. (2001). Teaching middle school students with learning disabilities to recruit peer assistance during cooperative learning group activities. *Learning Disabilities Research & Practice, 16,* 161–173.

Yunker, B. D. (1999). Adding authenticity to traditional multiple-choice test formats. *Education, 120,* 82–87.

Additional Readings

Abbott, M., Walton, C., & Greenwood, C. R. (2002). Phonemic awareness in kindergarten and first grade. *TEACHING Exceptional Children, 34*(4), 20–26.

Aber, M. E., Bachman, B., Campbell, P., & O'Malley, G. (1994). Improving instruction in elementary schools. *TEACHING Exceptional Children, 26*(3), 42–50.

Alberto, P. A., & Troutman, A. C. (2009). *Applied behavior analysis for teachers* (8th ed.). Upper Saddle River, NJ: Merrill/Prentice Hall.

Anhalt, K., McNeil, C. B., & Bahl, A. B. (1998). The ADHD classroom kit: A whole classroom approach for managing disruptive behavior. *Psychology in the Schools, 35*(1), 67–77.

Armstrong, D. C. (1994). Gifted child's education requires real dialogue: The use of interactive writing for collaborative education. *Gifted Child Quarterly, 38*, 136–145.

Arntz, A. (1993). Treatment of borderline personality disorder: A challenge for cognitive-behavioral therapy. *Behavioral Research Therapy, 32*, 419–430.

Arreaga-Mayer, C. (1998). Increasing active student responding and improving academic performance through class-wide peer tutoring. *Intervention in School and Clinic, 34*, 89–94.

Barkley, P. (1993). Eight principles to guide ADHD children. *The ADHD Report, 1*(2), 1–4.

Batshaw, M. L. (1997). *Children with disabilities* (4th ed.). Baltimore, MD: Brookes.

Bausch, M. E., & Ault, M. J. (2008). Assistive technology implementation plan: A tool for improving outcomes. *TEACHING Exceptional Children, 41*(1), 6–14.

Behrmann, M. M. (1994). Assistive technology for students with mild disabilities. *Intervention in School and Clinic, 30*(2), 70–82.

Behrmann, M. M. (1995). *Assistive technology for students with mild disabilities* (ERIC Digest E529). Reston, VA: Council for Exceptional Children. (ERIC Document Reproduction Service No. ED378755)

Behrmann, M. M., & Jerome, M. K. (2002). *Assistive technology for students with mild disabilities: Update 2002* (ERIC Digest E623). Arlington, VA: Council for Exceptional Children. (ERIC Document Reproduction Service No. ED463595)

Beirne-Smith, M. (1991). Peer tutoring in arithmetic for children with learning disabilities. *Exceptional Children, 57*, 330–337.

Belfiore, P. J., Grskovic, J. A., Murphy, A. M., & Zentall, S. S. (1996). The effects of antecedent color on reading for students with learning disabilities and co-occurring attention-deficit/hyperactivity disorder. *Journal of Learning Disabilities, 29*, 432–438.

Bender, W. N., & Shores, C. (2007). *Response to intervention: A practical guide for every teacher.* Thousand Oaks, CA: Corwin.

Bergan, J. R. (1977). *Behavioral consultation.* Columbus, OH: Merrill.

Bergman, A. B. (1993). Performance assessment for early childhood. *Science and Children, 30*(5), 20–22.

Beringer, V. W. (1997). Introduction to interventions for students with learning and behavior problems: Myths and realities. *School Psychology Review, 26*, 326–332.

Bernstorf, E. D., & Welsbacher, B. T. (1996). Helping students in the inclusive classroom. *Music Educators Journal, 82*, 21–37.

Biddulph, G., Hess, P., & Humes, R. (2006). Helping a child with learning challenges be successful in the general education classroom. *Intervention in School & Clinic, 41*, 315–316.

Birenbaum, M., & Feldman, R. A. (1998). Relationships between learning patterns and attitudes toward two assessment formats. *Educational Research, 40*, 90.

Bloom, B. S. (1986). Automaticity: The hands and feet of genius. *Educational Leadership, 43*(5), 70–77.

Bolocofsky, D. N. (1980). Motivational effects of classroom competition as a function of field dependence. *Journal of Educational Research, 73*, 213–217.

Bonus, M., & Riordan, L. (1998). *Increasing student on-task behavior through the use of specific seating arrangements.* (Master's Action Research Project). Chicago: Saint Xavier University. (ERIC Document Reproduction Service No. ED422129)

Bos, C. S., Mather, N., Silver-Pacuilla, H., & Narr, R. F. (2000). Learning to teach early literacy skills collaboratively. *TEACHING Exceptional Children, 32*(5), 38–45.

Bottage, B. A. (1999). Effects of contextualized math instruction on problem solving on average and below average achieving students. *Journal of Special Education, 33*, 81–92.

Bower, B. (1989). Remodeling the autistic child. *Science News, 136*, 312–313.

Bromley, K., & Mannix, D. (1993). Beyond the classroom: Publishing student work in magazines. *Reading Teacher, 47*, 72–77.

Browder, D. M., Ahlgrim-Delzell, L., Spooner, F., Mims, P. J., & Baker, J. N. (2009). Using time delay to teach literacy to students with severe developmental disabilities. *Exceptional Children, 75*, 343–363.

Browder, D. M., Wakeman, S. Y., Spooner, F., Ahlgrim-Delzell, L., & Algozzine, B. (2006). Research on reading instruction for individuals with significant cognitive disabilities. *Exceptional Children, 72*, 392–408.

Brulle, C. G. (1994). Elementary school student responses to teacher directions. *Education and Treatment of Children, 17*, 459–467.

Bryan, T., & Sullivan-Burstein, K. (1998). From behavior to constructivism in teacher education. *Remedial and Special Education Journal, 19*, 263–275.

Bryant, D. P., Bryant, B. R., Gersten, R., Scammacca, N., & Chavez, M. M. (2008). Mathematics intervention for first-and second-grade students with mathematics difficulties: The effects of Tier 2 intervention delivered as booster lessons. *Journal of Learning Disabilities, 29*, 20–32.

Bryant, P. E., Bradley, L., & Maclean, M. (1989). Nursery rhymes, phonological skills, and reading. *Journal of Child Language, 16*, 407–428.

Burns, B. (1999). *The mindful school: How to teach balanced reading and writing.* Upper Saddle River, NJ: Merrill/Prentice Hall.

Burns, B. (2000). *How to teach balanced reading and writing: The mindful school.* Upper Saddle River, NJ: Merrill/Prentice Hall.

Burns, M. S., Delclos, V. R., & Kulewicz, S. J. (1987). Effects of dynamic assessment on teachers' expectations of handicapped children. *American Educational Research Journal, 24*, 325–336.

Bursuck, W., Polloway, E. A., Plante, L., Epstein, M. H., Jayanthi, M., & McConeghy, J. (1996). Report card grading and adaptations: A national survey of classroom practices. *Exceptional Children, 62*, 301–305.

Bursuck, W. D., Munk, D. D., & Olson, M. M. (1999). The fairness of report card grading adaptations. *Remedial and Special Education, 20*(2), 84–90.

Burton, A. W., & Rodgerson, R. W. (2001). New perspectives on the assessment of movement skills and motor abilities. *Adapted Physical Activity Quarterly, 18*, 347–365.

Camoni, G. A., & McGeehan, L. (1997). Peer buddies: A child-to-child support program. *Principal, 76*, 40–43.

Campbell, P. S., & Scott-Kassner, C. (1995). *Music in childhood: From preschool through the elementary grades.* New York: Schirmer.

Capizzin, A. M. (2008). From assessment to annual goal: Engaging a decision-making process in writing measurable IEPs. *TEACHING Exceptional Children, 41*(1), 18–25.

Case-Smith, J. (1996). Half-pint smarts. *American Journal of Occupational Therapy, 49*, 39–40.

Cavalier, A., Ferretti, R. P., Hodges, A. E., Cavalier, A., Ferretti, R. P., & Hodges, A. E. (1997). Self-management within a classroom token economy for students with learning disabilities. *Research in Developmental Disabilities, 18*, 167–178.

Center for Applied Special Education (CAST). (2008). *Universal Design for Learning (UDL) guidelines: Version 1.0.* Retrieved April 19, 2009, from http://www.cast.org/publications/UDLguidelines/version1.html

Chandler, A. (1997). Is this for a grade? A personal look at journals. *English Journal, 86*, 45–49.

Chang, A. C. S., & Read, J. (2008). Reducing listening test anxiety through various forms of listening support. *TESL-EJ, 12*(1), 1–25.

Charney, R. S. (2002). *Teaching children to care: Classroom management for ethical and academic growth, K–8* (rev. ed.). Turners Falls, MA: Northeast Foundation for Children.

Chesapeake Institute. (1994). *Attention deficit disorder: What teachers should know.* Washington, DC: Division of Innovation and Development Office of Special Education Programs, Office of Special Education and Rehabilitative Services, U.S. Department of Education. (ERIC Document Reproduction Service No. ED370336)

Chesapeake Institute & Widmeyer Group. (1994). *101 ways to help children with ADD learn: Tips from successful teachers.* Washington, DC: Division of Innovation and Development, Office of Special Education Programs, Office of Special Education and Rehabilitative Services, U.S. Department of Education (ERIC Document Reproduction Service No. ED389109)

Cohen, M. (1993). Machines for thinking: The computer's role in schools. *Educational and Training Technology International, 30,* 57.

Cornoldi, C., Rigoni, F., Thessoldi, P. E., & Vio, C. (1999). Imagery deficits in nonverbal learning disabilities. *Journal of Learning Disabilities, 32,* 48–58.

Corral, N., & Antia, S. D. (1997). Self-talk: Strategies for success in math. *TEACHING Exceptional Children, 29,* 42–45.

Council for Exceptional Children. (2007). *CEC's position on response to intervention (RTI): The unique role of special education and special educators.* Available May 6, 2009, from http://www.cec.sped.org/AM/Template.cfm?Section=CEC_Professional_Policies&Template=/CM/ContentDisplay.cfm&ContentID=11116

Coyne, M. D., Sipoli, R. P., & Ruby, M. F. (2006). Beginning reading instruction for students at risk for reading disabilities: What, how, and when. *Intervention in School and Clinic, 41,* 161–168.

Crozier, S., & Tincani, M. J. (2005). Using a modified social story to decrease disruptive behavior of a child with autism. *Focus on Autism and Other Developmental Disabilities, 20,* 150–157.

Cunningham, P. (1998). How tutoring works. *Instructor, 107,* 36.

Dalton, B., Morocco, C., Tivnan, T., & Mead, P. R. (1997). Supported inquiry science: Teaching for conceptual change in urban and suburban science classrooms. *Journal of Learning Disabilities, 30,* 670–684.

Daniels, H., Zemelman, S., & Bizar, M. (1999). Whole language works: Sixty years of research. *Educational Leadership, 57*(2), 32–36.

de l'Etoile, S. (1996). Meeting the needs of the special learner in music. *American Music Teacher, 45,* 10–13.

De La Paz, S., & Graham, S., (1997). Strategy instruction in planning: Effects on the writing performance and behavior of students. *Exceptional Children, 63,* 167–181.

Desrochers, J. (1999). Vision problems: How teachers can help. *Young Children, 54*(2), 36–38.

Dockrell, J. E., Lindsay, G., Connelly, V., & Mackie, C. (2007). Constraints in the production of written text in children with specific language impairments. *Exceptional Children, 73,* 147–164.

Dollard, N., & Christensen, L. (1996). Constructive classroom management. *Focus on Exceptional Children, 29,* 1–11.

Dowd, J. (1997). Refusing to play the blame game. *Educational Leadership, 54,* 67–69.

Drueke, J., & Streckfuss, R. (1996). Some first steps in teaching a strategy for fact finding. *Journalism and Mass Communication Educator, 51*(2), 5–79.

Duffy-Hester, A. (1999). Teaching struggling readers in elementary school classrooms: A review of classroom reading programs and principles for instruction. *The Reading Teacher, 52,* 480–495.

Dumas, M. C. (1998). The risk of social interaction: Problems among adolescents with ADHD. *Education and Treatment of Children, 21,* 447–460.

Dunton, J. (1998). The four Bs of classroom management. *Techniques: Making Education and Career Connections, 73,* 32–33.

DuPaul, G. J., & Stoner, G. (1994). *ADHD in the schools: Assessment and intervention strategies.* NY: Guilford.

Eakin, S., & Douglas, V. (1971). Automatization and oral reading problems in children. *Journal of Learning Disabilities, 4,* 31–38.

Eastman, B. G., & Rasbury, W. C. (1981). Cognitive self-instruction for the control of impulsive classroom behavior: Ensuring the treatment package. *Journal of Abnormal Child Psychology, 93,* 381–387.

Educational Resources Information Center. (1998). *Teaching children with attention deficit/hyperactivity disorder.* Reston, VA: ERIC Clearinghouse on Disabilities and Gifted Education, Council for Exceptional Children. (ERIC Document Reproduction Service No. ED423633)

Edyburn, D. L. (2000). Assistive technology and students with mild disabilities. *Focus on Exceptional Children, 32*(9), 1–22.

Elischberger, H. B., & Roebers, C. M. (2001). Improving young children's free narratives about an observed event: The effects of nonspecific verbal prompts. *International Journal of Behavioral Development, 25,* 160–166.

Elksnin, L. (1997). Collaborative speech and language services for students with learning disabilities. *The Journal of Learning Disabilities, 30,* 414–426.

Enright, D. S., & Gomez, B. (1985). PRO-ACT: Six strategies for organizing peer interaction in elementary classrooms. *The Journal for the National Association for Bilingual Education, 9*(3), 5–24.

Erdmann, L. (1994). *Success at last.* Portsmouth, NH: Heinemann.

Espin, C. A., Shin, J., & Busch, T. W. (2005). Curriculum-based measurement in the content areas. *Journal of Learning Disabilities, 38,* 353–363.

Farrel, M., & John, E. (1995). Literacy for all? The case of Down syndrome. *Journal of Reading, 38,* 270–280.

Farrow, L. (1996). A quartet of success stories: How to make inclusion work. *Educational Leadership, 53*(5), 51–55.

Fleischner, J. E., & Manheimer, M. A. (1997). Math interventions for students with learning disabilities: Myths and realities. *School Psychology Review, 26,* 397–413.

Forgan, J. W., & Gonzales-DeHass, A. (2004). How to infuse social skills training into literacy instruction. *TEACHING Exceptional Children, 36*(6), 24–30.

Fowler, R. L. (1974). Effectiveness of highlighting for retention of text material. *Journal of Applied Psychology, 59,* 358–364.

Friar, K. K. (1999). Changing voices, changing times. *Music Educators Journal, 86*(3), 26–29.

Friedland, E. S., & Truesdell, K. S. (2006). "I can read to whoever wants to hear me read": Buddy readers speak out with confidence. *TEACHING Exceptional Children, 38*(5), 36–42.

Friend, M., & Bursuck, W. D. (2009). *Including students with special needs: A practical guide for teachers.* Boston: Allyn & Bacon.

Fuchs, D., Fuchs, L. S., & Compton, D. L. (2004). Identifying reading disabilities by responsiveness-to-instruction: Specifying measures and criteria. *Learning Disability Quarterly, 27,* 216–228.

Fuchs, D., Fuchs, L. S., McMaster, K. L., Yen, L., & Svenson, E. (2004). Nonresponders: How to find them? How to help them? What do they mean for special education? *TEACHING Exceptional Children, 37*(1), 72–77.

Fuchs, D., Fuchs, L. S., Thompson, A., Al Otaiba, S., Yen, L., Yang, N. J., et al. (2002). Exploring the importance of reading programs for kindergartners with disabilities in mainstream classrooms. *Exceptional Children, 68,* 295–311.

Fuchs, L. S., Compton, D. L., Fuchs, D., Paulsen, K., Bryant, J., & Hamlett, C. L. (2005). Responsiveness to intervention: Preventing and identifying mathematics disability. *TEACHING Exceptional Children, 37*(4), 60–63.

Fuchs, L. S., & Fuchs, D. (1998). General educators' instructional adaptation for students with learning disabilities. *Learning Disability Quarterly, 21,* 23–33.

Fuchs, L. S., Fuchs, D., & Compton, D. L. (2004). Monitoring early reading development in first grade: Word identification fluency versus nonsense word fluency. *Exceptional Children, 71,* 7–21.

Fuchs, L. S., Fuchs, D., Hamlett, C. L., Hope, S. K., Hollenbeck, K. N., Capizzi, A. M., et al. (2006). Extending responsiveness-to-intervention to math problem solving at third grade. *TEACHING Exceptional Children, 38*(4), 59–63.

Fuchs, L. S., Fuchs, D., Prentice, K., Burch, M., & Paulsen, K. (2002). Hot math: Promoting mathematical problem solving among third-grade students with disabilities. *TEACHING Exceptional Children, 35*(1), 70–73.

Fulk, B. M., Lohman, D., & Belfiore, P. J. (1997). Effects of integrated picture mnemonics on the letter recognition and letter-sound acquisition of transitional first-grade students with special needs. *Learning Disability Quarterly, 20,* 33–42.

Gallas, K. (1991). Arts as epistemology: Enabling children to know what they know. *Harvard Educational Review, 61,* 93–105.

Garcia, T. (2007). Facilitating the reading process. *TEACHING Exceptional Children, 39*(3), 12–17.

Gardill, M. C., DuPaul, G. J., & Kyle, K. E. (1996). Classroom strategies for managing students with attention-deficit/hyperactivity disorder. *Intervention in School and Clinic, 32,* 89–94.

Gately, S. E. (2004). Developing concept of word: The work of emergent readers. *TEACHING Exceptional Children, 36*(6), 16–22.

Geocaris, C., & Ross, M. (1999). A test worth taking. *Educational Leadership, 57*(1), 29–33.

Gerber, A., & Klein, E. R. (2004). A speech-language approach to early reading success. *TEACHING Exceptional Children, 36*(6), 8–14.

Getch, Y., Bhukhanwala, F., & Neuharth-Pritchett, S. (2007). Strategies for helping children with diabetes in elementary and middle schools. *TEACHING Exceptional Children, 39*(3), 46–51.

Gfeller, K. (1989). Behavior disorders: Strategies for the music teacher. *Music Educators Journal, 7,* 27–30.

Ghaziuddin, M., Leininger, L., & Tsai, L. (1995). Brief report: Thought disorder in Asperger syndrome; Comparison with high-functioning autism. *Journal of Autism and Developmental Disorders, 25,* 311–317.

Gibson, D., Haeberli, F. B., & Glover, T. A. (2005). Use of recommended and provided testing accommodations. *Assessment for Effective Intervention, 31,* 19–36.

Giordano, G. (1984). Analyzing and remediating writing disabilities. *Journal of Learning Disabilities, 17,* 78–83.

Glazer, S. M. (1998). Encouraging remarks. *Teaching PreK–8, 29,* 124–126.

Goolsby, T. W. (1999). Assessment in instrumental music. *Music Educators Journal, 95,* 31.

Graham, S., & Harris, K. R. (2006). Preventing writing difficulties: Providing additional handwriting and spelling instruction to at-risk children in first grade. *TEACHING Exceptional Children, 38*(5), 64–66.

Graham, S., Schwartz, S., & MacArthur, C. (1993). Knowledge of writing and the composing process, attitude toward writing, and self-efficiency for students with and without learning disabilities. *Journal of Learning Disabilities, 26,* 237–249.

Graves, M., & Graves, B. (1996). Scaffolding reading experiences for inclusive classes. *Educational Leadership, 53*(5), 14–16.

Griffin, L. L., & Butler, J. I. (Eds.). (2005). *Teaching games for understanding: Theory, research, and practice.* Champaign, IL: Human Kinetics.

Gunter, P. L., Denny, R. K., Jack, S. L., Shores, R. E., & Nelson, C. M. (1993). Aversive stimuli in academic interactions between students with serious emotional disturbance and their teachers. *Behavioral Disorders, 18,* 265.

Gunter, P. L., Denny, R. K., Jack, S. L., Shores, R. E., & Nelson, C. M. (1993). Aversive stimuli in academic interactions between students with serious emotional disturbance and their teachers. *Behavioral Disorders, 18*(4), 265–274.

Hankins, K. H. (1998). Cacophony to symphony: Memoirs in teacher research. *Harvard Educational Review, 68*(1), 80–95.

Harris, K. C., & Nevin, A. (1994). Developing and using collaborative bilingual special education teams. In Lilliam M. Malave (Ed.), *Annual Conference Journal, NABE '92–'93* (pp. 25–35). Washington, DC: National Association for Bilingual Education. (ERIC Document Reproduction Service No. ED372643)

Hebert, E. A. (1998). Lessons learned about student portfolios. *Phi Delta Kappan, 80,* 583–585.

Henderson, H. A., & Fox, N. (1998). Inhibited and uninhibited children: Challenges in school setting. *School Psychology Review, 27,* 492–505.

Herbert, E., & Schultz, L. (1996). The power of portfolios. *Educational Leadership, 53*(7), 70–71.

Hernandez, H. (1997). *Teaching in multicultural classrooms: A teacher's guide to context, process, and content.* New York: Simon and Schuster.

Higdon, H. (1999). Getting their attention. *Runner's World, 34,* 84.

Higgins, E. L., & Raskind, M. H. (1995). Compensatory effectiveness of speech recognition on the written composition performance of post-secondary students with learning disabilities. *Learning Disabilities Quarterly, 18,* 159–174.

Hitchcock, C. H., Prater, M. A., & Dowrick, P. W. (2004). Reading comprehension and fluency: Examining the effects of tutoring and video self-modeling on first-grade students with reading difficulties. *Learning Disability Quarterly, 27,* 89–103.

Holzberg, C. S. (1995). Beyond the printed book. *Technology and Learning, 15,* 22–23.

Huang, A., Mellblom, C., & Pearman, E. (1997). Inclusion of all students: Concerns and incentives of educators. *Education and Training in Mental Retardation and Developmental Disabilities, 32,* 11–20.

Huber, J. (1997). Laptop word processor: A way to close the technology gap. *Technology Connection, 4*(2), 26–28.

Humpal, M. E., & Dimmick, J. A. (1995). Special learners in the music classroom. *Music Educators Journal, 81,* 21–23.

Jackson, C. W., & Larkin, M. J. (2002). Rubrics: Teaching students to use grading rubrics. *TEACHING Exceptional Children, 35*(1), 40–45.

James, L. A., Abbot, M., & Greenwood, C. R. (2001). How Adam became a writer: Winning writing strategies for low-achieving students. *TEACHING Exceptional Children, 33*(3), 30–37.

Jitendra, A. K. (2002). Teaching students math problem-resolving through graphic representations. *TEACHING Exceptional Children, 34*(4), 34–38.

Jitendra, A. K., Rohena-Diaz, E., & Nolet, V. (1998). A dynamic curriculum-based language assessment. *Preventing School Failure, 42,* 182–185.

Johnson, D. (1990). Why can't my student learn like everyone else? *Adult Learning, 2*(2), 24–25, 28.

Johnson, G. M. (1999). Inclusive education: Fundamental instructional strategies and considerations. *Preventing School Failure, 43,* 72.

Johnson, K. K. (1998). Teaching Shakespeare to learning disabled students. *English Journal, 83,* 45.

Johnson, L., Graham, S., & Harris, K. R. (1997). The effects of goal setting and self-instruction on learning a reading comprehension strategy: A study of students with learning disabilities. *Journal of Learning Disabilities, 30,* 80–91.

Justice, L. M., & Kaderavek, J. (2002). Using shared storybook reading to promote emergent literacy. *TEACHING Exceptional Children, 34*(4), 8–13.

Kame'enui E. J., & Carnine, D. W. (1998). *Effective strategies that accommodate diverse learners.* Columbus, OH: Merrill/Prentice Hall.

Kelly, B., Hosp, J. L., & Howell, K. W. (2008). Curriculum-based math and evaluation: An overview. *Assessment for Effective Intervention, 33,* 250–256.

Kleinert, H. L., Kennedy, S., & Kearns, J. F. (1999). The impact of alternate assessments: A statewide teacher survey. *The Journal of Special Education, 33,* 93–102.

Kohn, A. (1996). Beyond discipline. *Education Week, 16,* 48.

Korinek, L. (1993). Positive behavior management: Fostering responsible student behavior. In B. S. Billingsley (Ed.; with D. Peterson, D. Bodkins, & M. B. Hendricks), *Program leadership for serving students with disabilities* (pp. 263–298). Blacksburg and Richmond: Virginia Polytechnic Institute and State University and Virginia State Department of Education. (ERIC Document Reproduction Service No. ED372537)

Kowalski, E., Lieberman, L., Pucci, G., & Mulawka, C. (2005). Implementing IEP or 504 goals and objectives into general physical education. *The Journal of Physical Education, Recreation & Dance, 76*(7), 33–37.

Kraayenoord, C. E., & Paris, S. G. (1997). Australian students' self-appraisal of their work samples and academic progress. *The Elementary School Journal, 97,* 523–527.

Kroeger, S. D., Burton, C., & Preston, C. (2009). Integrating evidence-based practices in middle science reading. *TEACHING Exceptional Children, 41*(3), 6–15.

Kroeger, S. D., & Kouche, B. (2006). Using peer-assisted learning strategies to increase response to intervention in inclusive middle math settings. *TEACHING Exceptional Children, 38*(5), 6–13.

Lambie, R. A. (1986). Adaptations for written expression. *Academic Therapy, 22,* 27–34.

Lane, K. L., Graham, S., Harris, K. R., & Weisenbach, J. L. (2006). Teaching writing strategies to young students struggling with writing and at risk for behavioral disorders: Self-regulated strategy development. *TEACHING Exceptional Children, 39*(1), 60–64.

Lee, D., & Gavine, D. (2003). Goal-setting and self-assessment in Year 7 students. *Educational Research, 45*(1), 49–59.

Lee, Y. J. (2006). The process-oriented ESL writing assessment: Promises and challenges. *Journal of Second Language Writing, 15,* 307–330.

Levy, N. R. (1996). Classroom strategies for managing students with attention-deficit/hyperactivity disorder. *Intervention in School and Clinic, 32*(2), 89–94.

Lewis, M., Wray, D., & Rospigliosi, P. (1994). Making reading for information more accessible to children with learning difficulties. *Support for Learning, 9,* 155–161.

Lewis, R. B. (1998). Assistive technology and learning disabilities: Today's realities and tomorrow's promises. *Journal of Learning Disabilities, 31,* 16–26.

Logan, K. R. (1998). Comparing instructional contexts of students with and without severe disabilities in general education classrooms. *Exceptional Children, 64*, 343–358.

Lombardi, T., & Butera, G. (1998). Mnemonics: Strengthening thinking skills of students with special needs. *The Clearing House, 71*, 284–287.

MacArthur, C., Graham, S., & Schwartz, S. (1995). Evaluation of a writing instruction model that integrated a process approach, strategy instruction, and word processing. *Learning Disability Quarterly, 18*, 278–294.

Macy, M. G., & Bricker, D. D. (2007). Embedding individualized social goals into routine activities in inclusive early childhood classrooms. *Early Child Development & Care, 177*, 107–120.

Majsterek, D. J. (1990). Writing disabilities: Is word processing the answer? *Intervention in School and Clinic, 26*(2), 93–97.

Malloy, W. (1997). Responsible inclusion: Celebrating diversity and academic excellence. *NASSP Bulletin, 81*, 80–85.

Manzo, A. V., Manzo, U. C., & Thomas, M. M. (2006). Rationale for systematic vocabulary development: Antidote for state mandates. *Journal of Adolescent & Adult Literacy, 49*, 610–619.

Marek-Schroer, M. F., & Schroer, N. A. (1993). Identifying and providing for musically gifted young children. *Roeper Review, 16*(1), 33–36.

Marjorie, M., & Applegate, B. (1993). Middle school students' mathematical problem-solving: An analysis of think-aloud protocols. *Learning Disability Quarterly, 16*, 19–30.

Martens, P. (1998). Using retrospective miscue analysis to inquire: Learning from Michael. *The Reading Teacher, 52*, 176–180.

Mastropieri, M. A., & Scruggs, T. E. (1997). Best practices in promoting reading comprehension in students with learning disabilities. *Remedial and Special Education, 18*, 197–213.

Mayer, G. R. (1999). Constructive discipline for school personnel. *Education and Treatment of Children, 22*, 36–54.

McEwan, E. K. (1998). *The ADHD intervention checklist.* Thousand Oaks, CA: Corwin.

McGrail, L. (1998). Modifying regular classroom curricula for high-ability students. *Gifted Child Today, 21*(2), 36–39.

McKinney, J. D., & Montague, M., & Hocutt, A. M. (1993). Educational assessment of students with ADD. *Exceptional Children, 60*, 125–133.

McLoughlin, J. A., & Lewis, R. B. (1994). *Assessing special students.* New York: Macmillan.

McNaughton, D. (1994). Spelling instruction for students with learning disabilities: Implications for research and practice. *Learning Disability Quarterly, 17*, 169–185.

McReynolds, J. C. (1988). Helping visually impaired students succeed in band. *Music Educators Journal, 71*, 35–38.

Meeks, L. L. (1999). Making English classrooms happier places to learn. *English Journal, 88*, 73–79.

Meisels, S. J. (1997). Using work sampling in authentic assessments. *Educational Leadership, 54*(4), 60–65.

Metzler, C. W., Biglan, A., Rusby, J. C., & Sprague, J. R. (2001). Evaluation of a comprehensive behavior management program to improve school-wide positive behavior support. *Education & Treatment of Children, 24*, 448–480.

Michaels, C. A., Brown, F., & Mirabella, N. (2005). Personal paradigm shifts in PBS experts: Perceptions of treatment acceptability of decelerative consequence-based behavioral procedures. *Journal of Positive Behavioral Supports, 7*, 93–108.

Miller, S. P., & Hudson, P. J. (2006). Helping students with disabilities understand what mathematics means. *TEACHING Exceptional Children, 39*(1), 28–35.

Moffatt, C. W., Hanley-Maxwell, C., & Donnellan, A. M. (1995). Discrimination of emotion, affective perspective-taking and empathy in individuals with mental retardation. *Education and Training in Mental Retardation and Developmental Disabilities, 30*, 76–84.

Monberg, G. H., & Monberg, L. Z. (2006). Classrooms and teaching space. *School Planning & Management, 45*(2), 56–57.

Montali, J., & Lewandowski, L. (1996). Bimodal reading: Benefits of a talking computer for average and less skilled readers. *Journal of Learning Disabilities, 29*, 271–279.

Montello, L., & Coons, E. E. (1998). Effects of active versus passive group music therapy on preadolescents with emotional, learning, and behavioral disorders. *Journal of Music Therapy, 35*(1), 49–67.

Monty, N. D. (1997). Transforming student assessment. *Phi Delta Kappan, 79,* 30–40, 58.

Moore, A. (1996). Assessing young readers: Questions of culture and ability. *Language Arts, 73,* 306–316.

Moran, M. R. (1987). Individualized objectives for writing instruction. *Topics in Language Disorders, 7,* 42–54.

Morgan, M., & Moni, K. B. (2005). Use phonics activities to motivate learners with difficulties. *Intervention in School and Clinic, 41*(1), 42–45.

Morgan, P. L., & Fuchs, D. (2007). Is there a bidirectional relationship between children's reading skills and reading motivation? *Exceptional Children, 73,* 165–183.

Moxley, R. A. (1998). Treatment-only designs and student self-recording as strategies for public school teachers. *Education and Treatment of Children, 21*(1), 37–61.

Mulcahy, C. A. (2008). The effects of a contextualized instructional package on the area and perimeter performance of secondary students with emotional and behavioral disabilities (Doctoral dissertation, University of Maryland, 2007). *Dissertation Abstracts International, 68,* 8-A.

Munk, D. D., & Bursuck, W. D. (1998). Can grades be helpful and fair? *Educational Leadership, 55,* 44.

Munk, D. D., & Bursuck, W. D. (2003). Grading students with disabilities. *Educational Leadership, 61*(2), 38–43.

Nagel, P. (2008). Moving beyond lecture: Cooperative learning and the secondary social studies classroom. *Education, 128,* 363–368.

National Board for Professional Teaching Standards. (2008). *The standards.* Retrieved April 19, 2009, from http://www.nbpts.org/the_standards/

National Institute of Mental Health (NIMH). (2004). National Institute of Mental Health multimodal treatment study of ADHD follow-up: 24-month outcomes of treatment strategies for attention-deficit/hyperactivity disorder. *Pediatrics, 113,* 754–761.

National Joint Committee on Learning Disabilities. (1993). Providing appropriate education for students with learning disabilities in regular education classrooms. *Journal of Learning Disabilities, 26,* 330–332.

NEO Direct. (2008). *AlphaSmartTM.* Retrieved April 19, 2009, from http://www.neo-direct.com

Newman, J. (1998). *Tensions of teaching: Beyond tips to critical reflection.* New York: Teachers College Press.

Niebling, B. C., & Elliott, S. N. (2005). Testing accommodations and inclusive assessment practices. *Assessment for Effective Intervention, 31*(1), 1–6.

Novelli, J. (1997). Seating solutions. *Primary Instructor, 107*(2), 78–79.

Olinghouse, N. G., Lambert, W., & Compton, D. L. (2006). Monitoring children with reading disabilities' response to phonics intervention: Are there differences between intervention aligned and general skill progress monitoring assessments? *Exceptional Children, 73,* 90–106.

Ormond, J. E. (1998). *Educational psychology: Developing learners* (2nd ed.). Upper Saddle River, NJ: Prentice Hall.

Ortiz, A. A. (1997). Learning disabilities occurring concomitantly with linguistic differences. *Journal of Learning Disabilities, 30,* 321–332.

Parette, H. P., Peterson-Karlan, G. R., Wojcik, B. W., & Bardi, N. (2007). Monitor that progress! Interpreting data trends for assistive technology decision making. *TEACHING Exceptional Children, 40*(1), 22–29.

Patzer, C. E., & Pettegrew, B. S. (1996). Finding a voice: Primary students with developmental disabilities express personal meanings through writing. *TEACHING Exceptional Children, 29*(2), 22–27.

Perry, L. A. (1997). Using wordless picture books with beginning readers (of any age). *TEACHING Exceptional Children, 29*(3), 68–69.

Pfiffner, L. J. (1998). *All about ADHD: The complete practical guide for classroom teachers.* New York: Scholastic.

Powell, S. (1995). When to intervene in selective mutism: The multimodal treatment of a case of persistent selective mutism. *Psychology in the Schools, 32,* 114–123.

Prater, M. A. (1992). Increasing time-on-task in the classroom. *Intervention in School and Clinic, 28*(1), 22–27.

Quinn, M. M., Gable, R. A., Rutherford, R. B., Nelson, C. M., & Howell, K. W. (1998). *Addressing student problem behavior: An IEP team's introduction to functional behavior assessment and behavior intervention plans* (2nd ed.). Washington, DC: American Institute for Research, Center for Effective Collaboration and Practice.

Raver, S. A. (2004). Monitoring child progress in early childhood special education settings. *TEACHING Exceptional Children, 36*(6), 52–57.

Reason, R. (1999). ADHD: A psychological response to an evolving concept. *Journal of Learning Disabilities, 32,* 85–91.

Reid, R. (1996). Research in self-monitoring with students with learning disabilities: The present, the prospects, the pitfalls. *Journal of Learning Disabilities, 29,* 317–331.

Reis, S. M., Burns, D. E., & Renzulli, J. S. (1995). *Curriculum compacting: The complete guide to modifying the regular curriculum for high ability students.* Mansfield Center, CT: Creative Learning Press.

Reis, S., & Renzulli, J. (1992). Using curriculum compacting to challenge the above-average. *Educational Leadership, 50,* 51–57.

Renzulli, J. S., & Reis, S. M. (1998). Talent development through curriculum differentiation. *NASSP Bulletin, 82,* 61–74.

Rhizzo, T., Faison-Hodge, J., Woodard, R., & Sayers, K. (2003). Factors affecting social experiences in inclusive physical education. *Adapted Physical Activity Quarterly, 20*(3), 317.

Riccomini, P. J. (2005). Identification and remediation of systematic error patterns in subtraction. *Learning Disability Quarterly, 28,* 233–242.

Rice, N., Drame, E., Owens, L., & Fattura, E. M. (2007). Co-instructing at the secondary level: Strategies for success. *TEACHING Exceptional Children, 39*(6), 12–18.

Richardson, C. (1990). Measuring musical giftedness. *Music Education Journal, 76,* 40.

Richardson, J. S. (2000). *Read it aloud: Using literature in the secondary content classroom.* Newark, DE: International Reading Association.

Riley, G., Beard, L. A., & Strain, J. (2004). Assistive technology at use in the teacher education programs at Jacksonville State University. *TechTrends: Linking Research & Practice to Improve Learning, 48*(6), 47–49.

Riley-Tilman, T. C., Chafouleas, S. M., & Briesch, A. M. (2007). A school practitioner's guide to using daily behavior report cards to monitor student behavior. *Psychology in the Schools, 44*(1), 77–89.

Ritchey, K. D. (2006). Learning to write: Progress-monitoring tolls for beginning and at-risk writers. *TEACHING Exceptional Children, 39*(2), 22–26.

Roberson, T. (1984). Determining curriculum content for the gifted. *Roeper Review, 6,* 137–139.

Robinson, M. (1995). Alternative assessment techniques for teachers. *Music Educators Journal, 81,* 28–34.

Rock, E. E., Fessler, M. A., & Church, R. P. (1997). The concomitance of learning disabilities and emotional/behavioral disorders: A conceptual model. *Journal of Learning Disabilities, 30,* 245–260.

Rodriguez, D., Parmar, R. S., & Signer, B. R. (2001). Fourth-grade culturally and linguistically diverse exceptional students' concepts of number line. *Exceptional Children, 67,* 199–210.

Rose, T. D. (1999). Middle school teachers: Using individualized instruction strategies. *Intervention in School and Clinic, 34*(3), 137–142.

Rosner, J. (1993). *Helping children overcome learning difficulties* (3rd ed.). New York: Walker.

Ruth, W. J. (1996). Goal setting and behavior contracting for students with emotional and behavioral difficulties. *Psychology in the Schools, 33,* 153–158.

Ryba, K., Selby, L., & Nolan, P. (1995). Computers empower students with special needs. *Educational Leadership, 53,* 82–84.

Saarimaki, P. (1995). Math in your world. *National Council of Teachers of Mathematics, 9,* 565–569.

Saddler, B., & Preschern, J. (2007). Improving sentence-writing ability through sentence-combining practice. *TEACHING Exceptional Children, 39*(3), 6–11.

Salend, S. (2009). Using technology to create and administer accessible tests. *TEACHING Exceptional Children, 41*(3), 40–51.

Salend, S., & Salend, S. J. (1985). Adapting teacher-made tests for mainstreamed students. *Journal of Learning Disabilities, 18,* 373–375.

Saudargas, R. A., & Zanolli, K. (1990). Momentary time sampling as an estimate of percentage time: A field violation. *Journal of Applied Behavior Analysis, 23,* 533–555.

Schirmer, B. R. (1987). Boosting reading success. *TEACHING Exceptional Children, 30*(1), 52–55.

Schlichter, C. L., & Brown, V. (1985). Application of the Renzulli model for the education of the gifted and talented to other categories of special education. *Remedial and Special Education, 6,* 49–55.

Schneiderman, R., & Werby, S. (1996). Homework improvement: A parent's guide to developing successful study habits in children before it's too late. (ERIC Document Reproduction Service No. ED414094)

Schoen, S. F., & Bullard, M. (2002). Action research during recess: A time for children with autism to play and learn. *TEACHING Exceptional Children, 35*(1), 36–39.

Schubert, A. (1997). I want to talk like everyone. *Mental Retardation, 35,* 347–354.

Shaaban, K. (2006). An initial study of the effects of cooperative learning on reading comprehension, vocabulary acquisition, and motivation to read. *Reading Psychology, 27,* 377–403.

Shapiro, E .S., DuPaul, G. J., & Bradley-Klug, K. L. (1998). Self-management as a strategy to improve the classroom behavior of adolescents with ADHD. *Journal of Learning Disabilities, 31,* 545–555.

Shenkle, A. M. (1989). Orchestrating the words. *Learning, 17*(5), 40–41.

Sherman, J. (1989). Yes (Virginia) we can see your story: Examining story elements in the drawing and writing of children. *Insights into Open Education, 22,* 17.

Shields, J., & Shealey, M. (1997). Educational computing gets powerful. *Technology and Learning, 18,* 20.

Shima, K., & Gsovski, B. K. (1996). Making a way for Diana. *Educational Leadership, 53,* 37–40.

Siege, L. S. (1995). Issues in the definition and diagnosis of learning disabilities: A perspective on *Guckenberger v. Boston University. Journal of Learning Disabilities, 32*(4), 304–319.

Siegel-Causey, E., & Allinger, R. M. (1998). Using alternative assessment for students with severe disabilities: Alignment with best practices. *Education and Training in Mental Retardation and Developmental Disabilities, 33,* 168–175.

Simmons, D. C., Fuchs, L. S., Fuchs, D., & Mathes, P. (1995). Effects of explicit teaching and peer tutoring on the reading achievement of learning disabled and low-performing students in regular classrooms. *Elementary School Journal, 95,* 387–408.

Simmons, D. C., Fuchs, L. S., Fuchs, D., Mathes, P., & Hodge, P. (1994). How inclusion built a community of learners. *Educational Leadership, 52,* 42–43.

Skau, L., & Cascella, P. W. (2006). Using assistive technology to foster speech and language skills at home and in preschool. *TEACHING Exceptional Children, 38*(6), 12–17.

Slavin, R. E. (1996). Neverstreaming: Preventing learning disabilities. *Educational Leadership, 53*(5), 4–7.

Smaligo, M. A. (1998). Resources for helping blind music students. *Music Educators Journal, 85,* 23–26.

Smith, S. B., Baker, S., & Oudeans, M. K. (2001). Making a difference in the classroom with early literacy instruction. *TEACHING Exceptional Children, 33*(6), 8–14.

Sprouse, C. A., Hall, C. W., Webster, R. E., & Bolen, L. M. (1998). Social perception in students with learning disabilities and attention deficit/hyperactivity disorder. *Journal of Nonverbal Behavior, 22,* 125–134.

Stauffer, S. L. (1999). Beginning assessment in elementary general music. *Music Educators Journal, 86,* 25–30.

Stenhoff, D. M., & Lignugaris, B. (2007). A review of the effects of peer tutoring on students with mild disabilities in secondary settings. *Exceptional Children, 74,* 8–30.

Stormont-Spurgin, M. (1997). I lost my homework: Strategies for improving organization in students with ADHD. *Intervention in School And Clinic, 32,* 270–274.

Sutman, F. X., et al. (1993). *Teaching science effectively to limited English proficient students* (ERIC/CUE Digest #87). New York: ERIC Clearinghouse on Urban Education. (ERIC Document Reproduction Service No. ED357113)

Swanson, P. (1998). Teaching effective comprehension strategies to students with learning and reading disabilities. *Intervention in School and Clinic, 33,* 209–218.

Taylor, H. E., & Larson, S. (1998). Teaching children with ADHD: What do elementary and middle school social studies teachers need to know. *Social Studies, 89,* 161–164.

Therrien, W. J., & Kubina, R. M. (2006). Developing reading fluency with repeated reading. *Intervention in School and Clinic, 41,* 15–160.

Thompson, A. (1996). Attention deficit hyperactivity disorder: A parent's perspective. *Phi Delta Kappan, 6,* 433–436.

Thompson, K. (1999). Internet resources in the general music classroom. *Music Educators Journal, 88,* 30–36.

Thompson, S. (1996). *Nonverbal learning disorders.* Retrieved April 19, 2009, from http://www.ldonline.org/article/6114/

Thurlow, M. L., Ysseldyke, J. E., & Silverstein, B. (1995). Testing accommodations for students with disabilities. *Remedial and Special Education, 16,* 260–270.

Tindal, G., & Parker, R. (1989). Assessment of written expression for students in compensatory and special education programs. *The Journal of Special Education, 23,* 169–183.

Tinzmann, M. B., Jones, B. F., Fennimore, T. F., Bakker, C. F., & Pierce, J. (1990). *What is the collaborative classroom?* Oak Brook, IL: North Central Regional Educational Laboratory (NCREL).

Torgesen, H. K., & Murphey, H. A. (1979). Verbal vs. nonverbal and complex vs. simple responses in the paired-associate learning of poor readers. *Journal of General Psychology, 101,* 219–226.

Tripp, A., Rizzo, T. L., & Webbert, L. (2007). Inclusion in physical education: Changing the culture. *The Journal of Physical Education, Recreation & Dance, 78*(2), 32–48.

Turnbull, A. P., Turnbull, R., & Wehmeyer, M. L. (2007). *Exceptional lives: Special education in today's schools* (5th ed.). Upper Saddle River, NJ: Pearson/Merrill Prentice Hall.

Uhry, J. K., & Shepard, M. J. (1997). Teaching phonological recoding to young children with phonological processing deficits: The effect on sight-vocabulary acquisition. *Learning Disability Quarterly, 20,* 104–125.

Vallecorsa, A. L., & deBettencourt, L. (1997). Using a mapping procedure to teach reading and writing skills to middle grade students with learning disabilities. *Education and Treatment of Children, 20,* 173–188.

van der Mars, H. (1994). Improving your instruction through self-evaluation (part 5): Assessing student behaviors. *Strategies, 7*(6), 26–29.

Vaughn, S., Elbaum, B., Schumm, J., & Hughes, M. (1998). Social outcomes for students with and without learning disabilities. *Journal of Learning Disabilities, 31,* 428–436.

Vaughn, S., Hughes, M. T., Schumm, J. S., & Klingner, J. (1998). A collaborative effort to enhance reading and writing instruction in inclusion classrooms. *Learning Disabilities Quarterly, 21,* 57–74.

Vaughn, S., Linan-Thompson, S., Kouzekanani, K., Bryant, D. P., Dickson, S., & Blozis, S. A. (2003). Reading instruction grouping for students with reading difficulties. *Remedial and Special Education, 24,* 301–315.

Voltz, D., Dooley, E., & Jeffries, P. (1999). Preparing special educators for cultural diversity: How far have we come. *Teacher Education and Special Education, 22,* 66–77.

Wadlington, E., Jacob, S., & Bailey, S. (1996). Teaching students with dyslexia in the regular classroom. *Childhood Education, 73,* 5.

Walczyk, E. B. (1993). Music instruction and the hearing impaired. *Music Educators Journal, 80,* 42–44.

Walker, L. M. (1993). Academic learning in an integrated setting for hearing-impaired students: A description of an Australian unit's efforts to meet the challenge. *The Volta Review, 95,* 295–304.

Ward-Lonergan, J. M., Liles, B. Z., & Owen, S. V. (1996). Contextual strategy instruction: Socially emotionally maladjusted adolescents with language impairments. *Journal of Communication Disorders, 29,* 107–124.

Webb-Johnson, G., Artiles, A., Trent, S., Jackson, C., & Velox, A. (1998). The status of research on multicultural education in teacher education and special education: Problems, pitfalls and promises. *Remedial and Special Education, 19,* 7–15.

Welsch, R. G. (2006). 20 ways to increase oral reading fluency. *Intervention in School and Clinic, 41,* 180–183.

Whitaker, S. D., Harvey, M., Hassell, L. J., Linder, T., & Tutterrow, D. (2006). The fish strategy: Moving from sight words to decoding. *TEACHING Exceptional Children, 38*(5), 14–18.

Williams, J. P. (2005). At-risk second graders can improve their comprehension of compare/contrast text. *TEACHING Exceptional Children, 37*(3), 58–61.

Williams, J. P., Hall, K. M., Lauer, K. D., & Lord, K. M. (2001). Helping elementary school children understand story themes. *TEACHING Exceptional Children, 33*(6), 75–77.

Willis, S. (1996). Managing today's classroom: Finding alternatives to control and compliance. *Education Update (Newsletter of the Association for Supervision and Curriculum Development), 38*(6), 1, 3–7.

Wilson, G. L. (2004). Using videotherapy to access curriculum and enhance growth. *TEACHING Exceptional Children, 36*(6), 32–37.

Wilson, R. (1996). Teachers building self-esteem in students. *The Delta Kappa Gamma Bulletin, 62,* 43–48.

Wirtz, C. L., Gardner, R., III, Weber, K., & Bullara, D. (1996). Using self-correction to improve the spelling performance of low-achieving third graders. *Remedial and Special Education, 17,* 48–58.

Wolery, M., Katzenmeyer, A. L., Snyder, E. D., & Werts, M. D. (1997). Training elementary teachers to embed instruction during classroom activities. *Education and Treatment of Children, 20*(1), 40–58.

Xin, Y. P., & Jittendra, A. K. (1999). The effects of instruction in solving mathematical word problems for students with special learning problems: A meta-analysis. *The Journal of Special Education, 32,* 207–225.

Yoo, S.-Y. (1997). Children's literature for developing good readers and writers in kindergarten. *Education/Print Source Plus, 118,* 123–128.

Ysseldyke, J. E., & Algozzine, B. (1995). *Special education: A practical approach for teachers* (3rd ed.). Boston: Houghton Mifflin.

Zadnik, D. (1992). *Instructional supervision in special education: Integrating teacher effectiveness research into model supervisory practices.* Bloomington: Indiana University, School of Education and Council of Administrators of Special Education. (ERIC Document Reproduction Service No. ED358646)

Zahorik, J. A. (1999). Reducing class size leads to individualized instruction. *Educational Leadership, 57*(1), 50–53.

Zentall, S. S., Smith, Y. N., Lee, Y. B., & Wieczorek, C. (1994). Mathematical outcomes of attention deficit hyperactivity disorder. *Journal of Learning Disabilities, 27,* 510–519.

Zhang, J. (2003). Effective instructional procedures for teaching individuals with severe disabilities in motor skills. *Perceptual & Motor Skills, 97,* 547–559.

Selected Internet Resources

RTI Accommodations/Modifications

The Council for Exceptional Children CEC): http://www.cec.sped.org

The Council for Exceptional Children (CEC) is the largest international professional organization dedicated to improving the educational success of individuals with disabilities and/or gifts and talents.

CEC advocates for appropriate governmental policies, sets professional standards, provides professional development, advocates for individuals with exceptionalities, and helps professionals obtain conditions and resources necessary for effective professional practice.

CEC provides the following services:

- Professional development opportunities and resources
- 17 divisions for specialized information
- Journals and newsletters with information on new research findings, classroom practices that work, federal legislation, and policies
- Conventions and conferences
- Special education publications

The Preparation to Practice Group (PPG): http://www.cehd.umn.edu

The Preparation to Practice Group (PPG) promotes a culture of professional learning and engagement concerning issues central to preK–12 professionals. Services span the continuum of development from initial preparation through professional practice. The PPG provides a model infrastructure to advance research, share knowledge, coordinate policy and practice, and collaborate with education partners to strengthen the profession and positively impact preK–12 student development.

The National Center to Improve Practice (NCIP): http://www2.edc.org/NCIP/

The National Center to Improve Practice (NCIP) was federally funded 1992–1998 to improve educational outcomes for students with disabilities by promoting the effective use of assistive and instructional technologies among educators and related personnel serving these students. Resources include the following:

- NCIP Library: A collection of resources about technology and special education
- Video Profiles: Videos of students using assistive and instructional technologies

- NCIP Guided Tours: Early Childhood: Hop on board the NCIP tour bus and explore two exemplary early childhood classrooms
- Spotlight on Voice Recognition: Explore the ins and outs of using voice recognition technology to address writing difficulties
- Online Workshops and Events: Archives of NCIP's online workshops and events held 1996–1998
- Links: Links to other special education and technology resources

Curriculum Online Resources for Educators (CORE): http://www.educationaltools.org/core/pdf/CORE_Special_Ed_Modifications.pdf

This resource from Curriculum Online Resources for Educators (CORE), by Educational Tools Inc., provides a list of common general education modifications and accommodations for students with special needs.

Accommodations: Assisting Students with Disabilities: A Guide for Educators: **http://eric.ed.gov (Search #ED444288.)**

This manual by Marty Beech (1999), describes different types of accommodations educators can use to include students with disabilities in general education classrooms, including accommodations relating to instructional methods and materials, assignments and classroom assessments, time demands and scheduling, learning environment, and use of special communication systems.

This Educational Resources Information Center (ERIC): http://eric.hoagiesgifted.org/e608.html

This Educational Resources Information Center (ERIC) digest by Cynthia Warger (2001) describes five strategies that researchers have identified to improve homework results for students with disabilities.

http://www.fldoe.org/ese/pdf/ac-mod-parents.pdf

From the Bureau of Instructional Support and Community Services of the Florida Department of Education and the Florida Developmental Disabilities Council, this is a guide for parents and caregivers regarding accommodations and modifications to instruction, assessment, the physical environment, behavior management, time management, communication systems, and collaboration strategies.

HIS Place for Help in School: http://www.hishelpinschool.com/adaptation/modadapt.html

This page at the HIS Place for Help in School Web site, by the Home Educators Association of Virginia, is a guide to promoting the understanding of accommodations and modifications to instruction and assessment.

http://www-01.ibm.com/software/awdtools/tester/policy/accessibility/

This software product from IBM, Rational Policy Tester (Accessibility Edition), ensures Web site user accessibility by monitoring over 170 accessibility checks and determining a site's level of compliance with government standards.

The IRIS Center: http://iris.peabody.vanderbilt.edu

The IRIS Center provides high-quality resources for college and university faculty and professional development providers about students with disabilities. IRIS seeks to achieve this goal by providing free, online, interactive training enhancements that translate research about the education of students with disabilities into practice.

The Access Center: http://www.k8accesscenter.org

The Access Center offers resources that focus on core content areas—language arts, math, and science—as well as on instructional and learning strategies to provide students with disabilities access to rigorous academic content. In addition, there are professional development modules and information briefs on such topics as teaching and learning strategies, media and materials, supports and accommodations, universal design for learning, differentiated instruction, and collaborative teaching.

The Learning Disabilities Association of America (LDA): http://www.ldanatl.org

The Learning Disabilities Association of America (LDA) provides cutting-edge information on learning disabilities, practical solutions, and a comprehensive network of resources. Learning disabilities include dyslexia, dyscalculia, and dysgraphia and are often complicated by associated disorders, such as attention deficit/hyperactivity disorder (ADHD).

LD OnLine: http://www.ldonline.org/indepth/accommodations/

LD OnLine provides information and advice about learning disabilities and ADHD for teachers, parents, and other professionals. The site features hundreds of helpful articles, multimedia resources, and monthly columns by noted experts; first-person essays and children's writing and artwork; a comprehensive resource guide; very active forums; and a Yellow Pages referral directory of professionals, schools, and products.

http://www.ldonline.org/article/c682/

This section of the LD OnLine Web site contains articles that provide helpful information about 504 plans and various types of accommodations.

The National Center for Learning Disabilities (NCLD): http://www.ncld.org/content/view/348/346/

The National Center for Learning Disabilities (NCLD) provides information and resources for parents, educators, and other professionals regarding learning disabilities.

The National Dissemination Center for Children with Disabilities (NICHCY): http://www.nichcy.org/EducateChildren/Supports/Pages/default.aspx

The National Dissemination Center for Children with Disabilities (NICHCY) provides information regarding accommodation, adaptations, and modifications for children with disabilities.

The Office of Special Education Programs (OSEP): http://osepideasthatwork.org

The Office of Special Education Programs (OSEP) is dedicated to improving results for infants, toddlers, children, and youth with disabilities. OSEP, directly and through its partners and grantees, develops a wide range of research-based products, publications, and resources to assist states, local district personnel, and families to improve results for students with disabilities. This Web site provides easy access to information from research-to-practice initiatives funded by OSEP that address the provisions of Individuals with Disabilities Education Act (IDEA) and NCLB. It includes resources, links, and other important information that supports OSEP's research-to-practice efforts.

On the Same Team: http://www.specialedmoms.com/accommodations.html

This Web site by On the Same Team provides information and resources regarding accommodations and medications.

Journal of Special Education Technology (JSET): **http://www.tamcec.org/jset/index/index.htm**

JSET, or the *Journal of Special Education Technology,* is a refereed professional journal that presents up-to-date information and opinions about issues, research, policy, and practice related to the use of technology in the field of special education. JSET supports the publication of research and development activities, provides technological information and resources, and presents important information and discussion concerning issues in the field of special education technology to scholars, teacher educators, and practitioners.

The Treatment and Learning Centers (TLC):
http://www.ttlc.org/Web%20Resource%20Library/Common%20Testing%20Accommodations.pdf

This "Super Duper Handy Handout" from the Treatment and Learning Centers (TLC) provides a discussion of accommodations and modifications for students with disabilities.

Index

CORWIN

A SAGE Company

The Corwin logo—a raven striding across an open book—represents the union of courage and learning. Corwin is committed to improving education for all learners by publishing books and other professional development resources for those serving the field of PreK–12 education. By providing practical, hands-on materials, Corwin continues to carry out the promise of its motto: **"Helping Educators Do Their Work Better."**